Understanding American Culture

The Theological and Philosophical Shaping of the American Worldview

Glenn Rogers

Published by

Mission and Ministry Resources
Bedford, Texas

www.missionandministryresources.net

TABLE OF CONTENTS

Introduction

This book is about understanding the forces that shaped American culture, making Americans who they are. To understand why Americans are they way they are requires that we take a journey through history to discover what forces, circumstances, and events shaped the cultural contexts that eventually shaped the American worldview.

To do this, we have to start in a cultural context far removed from Western Europe and the people who would come to American in search of freedom and opportunity. To understand the shaping of the West and of America, we have to start in the Ancient Middle East, in what today would be Iraq, with a man named Abram.

In addition to Abram and the impact his ancestors (the Israelites) and their religion (Judaism) had on Western culture, the ancient Greeks require considerable attention for their role in shaping Western thinking. Then, of course, Jesus and Christianity must be factored in. Why? For this simple reason: to understand Western people and their culture, one must understand the dynamic tension that has existed between religion, especially Christianity, and philosophy in the shaping of Western Europe and, eventually, America.

To understand Western culture one must have a sense of the uneasy interplay between religion and philosophy and the impact that each had, independently and in combination, on politics, war, economics, investigation and discovery, perspective and perception, exploration and expansion, and the intellectual and emotional development of a people whose cultural roots are buried deep in the soil of ancient Greece and Rome, nourished by a spiritual river that flows out of ancient Canaan and Palestine.

To accomplish this historical overview of the development of Western culture we will examine the concept of culture as well as eight significant periods of time and related events of that have shaped Western culture:

1. The Development of Ancient Israel and the Jewish Religion
2. The Development of Greek Culture, Philosophy and Science
3. The Development and Expansion of Christianity
4. The Collapse of the Empire, the Rise of the Church
5. The Renaissance
6. The Enlightenment
7. The Founding of American
8. Contemporary American Culture

Before we start down that path, however, it is necessary to discuss some other matters. We can't really understand much about Western culture until we understand the concept of culture in general. What is culture? Where does it come from? How does it work? What impact does it have on people? And of course, to understand culture we must understand worldview. What is worldview and how does it work? What is the relation between worldview and culture?

Our study, then, will be divided into two main sections: Part One, Culture, and Part Two, Western Culture.

One final note before we begin: history buffs who are familiar with traditional historical presentations of the development of Western Civilization may question the importance I have given to Judeo-Christian forces in shaping the American worldview. Before I began to restudy the matter I would have questioned it as well. We tend to question things we haven't heard before. That, of course, causes one to wonder why we have not heard more regarding the role of Christianity in the shaping of Western civilization. Why historians have not given the subject adequate attention is not for me to say. Normally they explain what happened, when and where and, from a surface-level perspective, why things may have happened. But rarely do they examine the deep-level, underlying assumptions that may have shaped what happened. The history, however, is there if one is willing to look at it.

Part 1

Culture

Chapter 1

What Is Culture

Defining Culture

In 1871 E. B. Tylor defined culture as that "*complex whole which includes knowledge, belief, art, morals, law, customs, and any other capabilities and habits acquired by man as a member of society*," (Carrithers 1997:98). Anthropologists today still refer to this early definition of culture. Paul Hiebert's definition is a little less cumbersome: "*the integrated system of learned patterns of behavior, ideas, and products characteristics of a society*," (1983:25).

Culture is a complex whole, an integrated system. It involves beliefs, ideas, knowledge, behaviors, morals (values), laws, customs, habits and more. Culture is basically everything about a group of people. Culture is the way a people live their lives. It involves the actual things they do and the way they do them; how they: eat, sleep, dress, get married, work, play, have babies, raise children, bury their dead, dance, worship, buy, sell, trade, think, teach, learn, mourn, laugh, fight, relax—everything people do and how they do it is part of their culture. So are the ideas and assumptions about life that result in what a people do and how they do it.

Analyzing Culture

That culture involves the assumptions and beliefs that lead to behaviors as well as the behaviors themselves means that there is more than one level to culture. In fact, there are at least three levels to every society's culture. Culture is a three-tiered phenomenon made up 1) of our *deep-level* assumptions about the world and about how life is to be lived (called *worldview*), 2) of our *mid-level* internal values and our ways of feeling and thinking that grow out of our deep-level worldview assumptions, and 3) of our *surface-level* behaviors and structures. Figure 1 illustrates this three-tiered view of culture. Take a moment to study it.

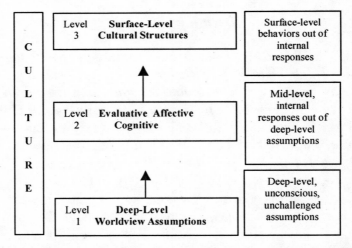

FIGURE 1: THREE-TIERED VIEW OF CULTURE
(Rogers 2002:42, 2006:40)

Level-three, surface-level cultural structures and behaviors, is that part of culture that we see and experience with our senses. Surface-level culture is external. It is what we eat, how we dress, drive a car, go to the bank, grocery shop, go to a movie, vote—all the things we do as we live life. These are our cultural behaviors. Cultural structures are the institutions we create that provide a framework for daily living: schools for educating our children, hospitals for caring for the sick. Our economic system is a cultural institution, so is marriage. Democracy is a cultural institution.

Surface-level institutions and behaviors are related. If democracy is a cultural institution, voting is a cultural behavior. If our educational system is a cultural institution, sending our children to school is a cultural behavior. If capitalism is a cultural institution, buying a car is a cultural behavior. Our cultural behaviors are often accomplished in relation to a cultural structure. The cultural structures provide a context or framework for cultural behaviors. Structures and behaviors are the visible parts of our culture.

Level-two, mid-level internal responses, are the values, feelings, and thinking that lay just beneath the surface of behaviors and structures. In the West, we teach our children that cheating on a test is wrong. That is a cultural behavior we engage in. Why do we do that? Because we believe cheating is wrong. Our behaviors grow out of our values, our feelings, our thinking. When we have a headache we take medicine designed to produce a specific chemical reaction in our bodies to reduce or eliminate the pain in our heads. Why would we do that? In some other cultures a person might go to a witch doctor to have a curse removed that he or she believes is causing the head ache. Why would our surface-level cultural behavior be different from that of other cultural groups? Because our mid-level internal responses are different. We have different values. We think differently; we feel differently about things. The way we think and feel about things determines how we behave.

Our mid-level internal responses drive our surface-level behaviors and the structures we have created in relation to them. Level-two determines level-three. But where do

12

these level-two values, feelings, and thinking come from? I have called them mid-level internal *responses*—responses to what? Our mid-level internal values, feelings, and thinking develop in response to our deep-level (level-one) unconscious assumptions about reality, about how life ought to be lived. These deep-level assumptions are referred to as *worldview.*

Worldview as the Foundation of Culture

The word *worldview* is used rather freely to refer to all sorts of things. This is unfortunate because when a word means too many things it does not really mean anything very specific. Usually when people use the word worldview they mean perspective. Often they are thinking of a particular philosophical or theological perspective or point of view. Their communication would be more accurate if they would simply use the word perspective.

Worldview, as it us used anthropologically, is a very precise term that refers to the deep-level unconscious assumptions a people have about reality, about the nature of the world and about how life is to be lived (Kraft 1996:52). Worldview, whether on the individual level or the societal level, allows people to understand themselves in relation to the world, and provides them with a framework for interpreting and living life.

To understand how worldview is part of culture and how it factors into the larger issue of understanding Western culture we must examine it more thoroughly.

What is Worldview[1]

Worldview is *the unconscious, deep-level assumptions people have about reality as they perceive it; assumptions about how the world works and how to relate to and interact with all the things, events and people encountered in life* (Rogers 2002:27).

Worldview is, for most people, an unconscious feature of who they are. Most people are not even aware of their deep-level assumptions about reality. Hiebert has noted that worldview is "what we think with, not what we think about" (1996:142). I will elaborate on the *"what we think with"* part of his comment later. For now the point is that people are unaware of their underlying assumptions about reality.

As children we learn our worldview as we grow. We learn it in our specific social and cultural context. Actually, the word *absorb* may be a better word to describe the process. We do not learn our worldview the way we learn the multiplication tables. No one sits us down to teach us worldview. For the most part, worldview is *transmitted* to us informally and unintentionally within our cultural context as we listen to and observe our parents or other significant people in our lives. As we listen, observe, and experience we learn and form impressions about living life in our cultural context. On those occasions when our parents specifically instruct us, *this is what we believe and this is what we do*, we are being intentionally taught and portions of our worldview are being formed, but seldom is the word worldview used.

The impressions we form as we grow become assumptions about life. We do not question these assumptions. We simply accept them. For instance, if we

---

[1] For a fuller discussion of the development of worldview studies and theory from an anthropological perspective, see Rogers 2002:9-65.

grow up in a family that prays to God, we accept the idea of God without questioning it. We hear our parents talking to God and we hear the kinds of things they thank him for and ask him to do and we form impressions that become assumptions about an invisible, all-powerful being who is actively involved in his world and who cares about and intervenes in the lives of people. As children we cannot articulate our assumptions in theological terms, but the assumptions are there. It does not occur to us to question our assumptions about God because that is the nature of assumptions—we simply assume them to be true.

We do not often think about our deep-level assumptions about life so they remain *unconscious*. For instance, if you ask the average American about his assumptions regarding time, he will not be able to tell you. This is not because he doesn't think about time. Americans think about time all the time! But most of us do not think about our *assumptions* regarding time. We don't think about how we perceive time, why we think of it the way we do, which is different from the way other people in the world think about time. Most people don't spend a lot of time thinking about their deep-level worldview assumptions.

These deep-level worldview assumptions are about our *perceptions of reality*, assumptions about how the world works and about how life is to be lived. Our assumptions about the nature of reality have to do with a number of important and very basic considerations. What is the world like? How does it work? And, most importantly, what is my place in it? Because humans, by nature, are very focused on themselves, questions about how the world works are rooted in the basic *Self-Other* dichotomy. There is me (*Self*) and there is everything and everyone else (*Other*). What is my relationship with every thing and every one else? What is the relationship of the *Self* to the *Other*? Figure 2 illustrates this *Self-Other* dichotomy.

15

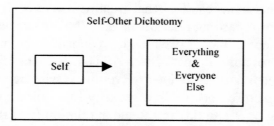

FIGURE 2: SELF-OTHER DICHOTOMY

Within the framework of this basic *Self-Other* dichotomy, lots of questions are asked and answered. The answers exist in the form of assumptions we develop as our worldview is being formed. The questions are not always framed in the context of the *Self*, but the *Self* is always present in the background. For instance, instead of asking, w*hy do things happen to me,* we may simply ask, w*hy do things happen.* Our presence in the scenario is understood even if not specified, and the more generalized inquiry has broad implications.

The question is one of causality. It is an inquiry into the nature of the world. Why do things happen? Do things happen because a personal being (God or gods and spirits) make them happen? Or do things happen because impersonal forces (laws of physics) generate cause and effect actions and reactions? When it rains too much and there is a flood and people die, did someone cause that to happen or did it just happen? Did God cause the flood, or is global warming to blame?

As children we do not puzzle through these difficult questions in any kind of sophisticated formal manner. We simply form impressions and develop assumptions based on the way our parents and others around us react to the challenges of life.

Another example of how we work out the *Self-Other* dichotomy as we form our worldview assumptions about life is in the area of relationships. By the way we are treated and how we feel as a result of that treatment, we begin to form impressions regarding relationships. Who are the people that are important to me? To whom do I appear to be important? Mother probably comes first. Then perhaps father, or another secondary caregiver. Eventually siblings will/may enter the picture and we find security (assuming everything is working as it should) in the close relationships of family. That family may be the nuclear family, parents and children, or the extended family, grandparents, aunts, uncles, cousins—everybody that can be classified as "my people."

These are just a couple of examples of the kinds of basic questions/assumptions that are involved in worldview. The sections that follow will include more detail about how worldview works and how a people's worldview assumptions provide the foundation of their culture. For now it is important to focus on the idea that worldview is the deep-level, unconscious assumptions a person has (or a people have) about reality, about how the world works and their place in it. These assumptions impact us in profound ways as we live life. Our deep-level assumptions (level-one) grow into the mid-level internal values, feelings and thinking (level-two) that drive the surface-level (level-three) behaviors that characterize our culture.

Worldview Universals

Worldview assumptions can be divided into five basic categories called *universals*. They are called universals because all groups of people have assumptions about these basic life considerations. These universal categories include: causality, classification, relationship, orientation to space, and orientation to time.

Causality—assumptions about why things happen, forces or powers in the cosmos that are somehow involved in the unfolding of day-to-day life. Are these forces or powers impersonal forces (such as gravity) beyond the influence of humans? Or are they personal beings whose choices and powers can be influenced by human beings? If the "forces" are impersonal forces beyond the influence of humans, how do we cope with the events they cause? If the "powers" are personal beings that humans can influence, how do go about influencing them in order to achieve the desired result? These are the kinds of questions/assumptions involved in the worldview universal category of causality.

Classification—assumptions about how things are related, how all things in life are categorized in relation to everything else. Why would some people put an orange, a chicken's foot, and a monkey into the same category? Because for some people all three of those things are food. The way we classify people and things depends on our worldview assumptions. I would not classify my wife or children as part of the property I own. Many men from traditional societies would. In my way of classifying things that happen in the world I have a category for "accidents" and another for "random occurrences." Many people in the world do not have an "accidents" or "random occurrences" category, because for them there are no such things as accidents or random occurrences. For those people, things happen because someone (perhaps God, or a spirit or an ancestor) made them happen. Assumptions about how things are related to one another and how things are associated with and grouped together are related to the worldview universal category of classification.

Relationship—assumptions about our self and the kind of relationships we sustain with those around us. Am I first and foremost an individual whose primary identity and value grow out of the simple fact that I exist? Or am I first and foremost part of a group of people with my identity and value growing out of my relationship with and to that group? And do I view others primarily as individuals or as members of a group—either my group or not my group? If my assumptions about how life is to be lived are rooted in a group orientation, who is part of my group and who is not part of my group? Who is community and who is not? If my worldview assumptions are rooted in an individual orientation, what level of autonomy is required? How can I be an individual and still be part of a family group? Who comes first, the group or me? How does a group that is made up of "individuals" function differently than a group of people who are primarily members of a group? How are decisions made? How are freedom and responsibility factored in? These kinds of questions, *"how do I relate to other people,"* fall into the Relationship universal of worldview assumptions.

Orientation to space—assumptions related to how I think about the space I occupy, my relationship to the world, to nature, to things—my place in the world. Am I part of the space I occupy or separate from it? Do I own it, use it, manage it? Is there a space in the world that is mine or do I share the space I occupy with other people? Do I share it with all other people or only with those who are my people? How should space (mine or ours) be organized? Should it be specialized and compartmentalized or used holistically? Should buildings be round or angular? Should there be private property or should there be community sharing of all resources? Does my orientation start with myself and go outward to other people and things, or does it begin outwardly with other people and things and move inward toward me?

For instance, a person with an orientation that starts with himself and goes outward who is walking from north to south and who passes a tree will think in terms of the tree as being is on his right. His orientation is himself. He perceives his world by his presence in it. On his return walk, now going south, he will think in terms of the tree being on his left. This person thinks of the world (the space he occupies) from a *self-central-focus*. He is the central focus. The world exists in relation to himself. A person with a *world-central-focus* making the same trips past the tree would think of the tree as the central feature, an enduring part of the bigger picture that is the point of reference rather than the individual (Kearney 1983:161-164). A self-central-focus and a world-central-focus represent two very different orientations to the space we occupy, the world we live in.

These are the kinds of questions related to the worldview universal of orientation to space.

Orientation to time—assumptions regarding how time works and how we think about it and use time. Is time like a river that flows out of the past, into the present and on into the future? Or is time like a circle of recurring events from season to season and generation to generation? If time can be compared to a tree, am I focused on the roots that reach into the past, on the trunk that is a substantial representation of the very solid present, or on the branches that reach up toward a future that is yet to unfold? Do I live my life with a past, present, or future orientation? Is life to be thought of as an ongoing series of events and relationships that occur as they unfold, moments that vary in duration and quality? Or is life to be viewed as moments to be calculated, organized, measured, and managed? Western people will answer these questions differently than non-Western people.

Which is the more important concern for most Americans, what has happened in the past, or what may happen in the future? The present is real. The future is not yet real. How much of the present should I devote to an attempt to impact a future that is not yet real and that may not become real? Am I more concerned with the quality of an event and the relationships that are created or nourished by the event? Or am I more concerned with the timeframe in which the events occur? Is it more important to be focused on where you are or where you are going to be? In the living of life and the passing of days are there relationships to be enjoyed or schedules to be kept? Is the passage of time equated with the quality of life or with productivity and profit?

Our Western orientation to time is not usually an all or nothing approach with punctually, for example, winning out over relationships. For instance, most Americans will tell you that relationships are more important than punctuality. However, when you observe how they behave it is apparent that punctuality is often given priority over relationships. For example, a wife calls her husband at work to discuss a matter with him. He explains that he has a meeting in ten minutes and needs to pull together his notes and files. Can they discuss the matter later? Which was more important, talking to his wife or getting to the meeting fully prepared on time? The way Americans behave illustrates their true beliefs about time and how it is to be managed.

Each of these five worldview universal categories involves a number of significant and complex questions and issues that have serious implications for how we live life. Figure 3 is a diagram of worldview universals.

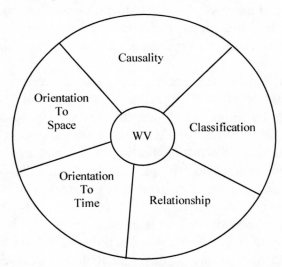

FIGURE 3: WORLDVIEW UNIVERSALS

21

Worldview as a Reality Filter

Our worldview serves as a reality filter. Everything we encounter in life, all the reality that we experience, gets filtered through our worldview. There is nothing that we encounter or experience (physically, emotively, cognitively) that is not experienced, judge, categorized, and responded to on the basis of our worldview assumptions. If an experience makes us happy, sad, or angry, trace the emotion back far enough (or deep enough) and you will find an assumption in one of the worldview universals involved in that emotion. Our actions and reactions, our values, our thinking and our feelings all grow out of our worldview assumptions. As we live life, our worldview assumptions (without our awareness of the process) are guiding us in how we react to that which we encounter or experience.

When we determine a thing is or is not worth our time or attention, several layers down, deep below our conscious level of awareness, our worldview is at work. Our worldview informs our value system, which in turn, tells us whether or not a thing is worth our time or attention. All of the hundreds of questions and possible responses related to worldview universals get answered based on our worldview assumptions. Our assumptions regarding the relative importance of *harmony* versus *justice* will guide and inform our decision to seek reconciliation or discover blame and accountability. Our assumptions regarding causality (impersonal forces such as physics versus a personal being such as God, or some combination of the two) informs our thinking and feelings when we hear that hundreds or thousands of people have died in an earthquake or as a result of a volcanic eruption.

Life is lived on the basis of how experiences are filtered though our worldview. People everywhere in the world experience the same basic REALITY. But REALITY is individually and culturally perceived. The word

22

REALITY (written in all capital letters) represents the real actual REALITY that people experience, while the word reality (written in small case letters) represents the individual and cultural perception of REALITY.

All people live in the same world, have the same physical needs and experience the same general life experiences: birth, hunger, heat, cold, fear, joy, sickness, aloneness, love, betrayal, anger, thirst, exhaustion, age, death. The same REALITY comes to us all. But what comes to us as REALITY is filtered through our culturally impacted worldview and comes out as reality—our reality, a reality shaped, understood and dealt with on the basis of our worldview. REALITY becomes reality as it passes through our worldviews. This happens on an individual level. But if enough people in a given society share very similar worldview assumptions, the process then occurs on a societal or cultural level[2].

Figure 4 illustrates how different worldviews (on the societal level not the individual level), acting as *experience filters*, impact how a society experiences and interprets REALITY. Differing interpretations of REALITY result in different cultural expression of reality.

Worldview as an Interpretive Framework for Life

Not only does our worldview filter REALITY for us, in doing so it provides us with a framework for effective living, that is, for making sense out of life's experiences (Kraft 2002:7.1-17). How does one cope with the death of a loved one, with the tragedy of a deadly tornado, with the loss of a job, with social injustice, with shattered dreams, with betrayal, defeat, frustration, with the price of gasoline and of milk? How does one cope with victory, with the realization

---

[2] I am indebted to Charles Kraft for this REALITY/reality way of explaining perception (1996: 17-20).

of dreams, with being in the right place at the right time, with a good income and a healthy family, with a good

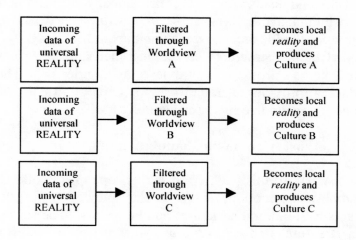

FIGURE 4: WORLDVIEW AS A REALITY FILTER
(Rogers 2002:56)

education and leisure time, with a good retirement fund, a nice house, nice cars, nice, clothes, good food and good friends and nice restaurants? How does one cope with the good one enjoys while so many others do not? How does one cope with so much suffering when so many others do not have to?

Worldview assumptions help us make sense of these kinds of challenging questions—even if the answer we come up with is simply, *"It's the luck of the draw."* Worldview is at work in that answer. Whether or not the assumptions that would lead one to that conclusion are valid is another matter altogether, but worldview assumptions provide the basis for such conclusions. Our level-one worldview assumptions are the basis for our level-two internal responses (values, feelings, thinking), which are the basis for our level-three cultural structures and behaviors. The kind of funerals we have, for instance, and the way we act at funerals, traces its way back down the chain to our worldview assumptions about life and death. As Hiebert has noted, worldview is not what we think about, but *what we think with*. Our worldview assumptions guide us in how we think about life.

Cultural structures are coping mechanisms that are rooted in a people's worldview assumptions. Thus, worldview provides a framework for coping with life, for living effectively in one's social context.

Worldview as the Foundation of Culture

What all this adds up to is that a people's collective worldview assumptions serve as the foundation for their surface-level cultural structures and behaviors. The surface-level structures and behaviors are what we see. The deep-level assumptions are buried deep in the collective unconscious of the community and are not readily apparent. Just as the foundation of a building is part of the building, but is underneath and out of sight, so worldview is a part of a people's culture but is underneath and out of sight.

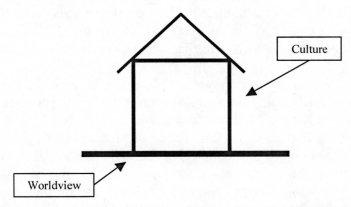

Figure 5: Worldview as the Foundation of Culture

Given the role worldview plays in people's lives, it is clear that if you want to understand a group of people, if you want to know why they are the way they are, you must understand their worldview. To understand American culture, to understand why Americans are they way they are (even if you are an American) you must understand the basic features of a Western worldview.

Summary

Culture is *"the integrated system of learned patterns of behavior, ideas, and products characteristic of a society,"* (Hiebert 1983:25). Culture is a three-tiered phenomenon made up 1) of our *deep-level* assumptions about the world and about how life is to be lived (called *worldview*), 2) of our *mid-level* internal values and our ways of feeling and thinking that grow out of our deep-level worldview assumptions, and 3) of our *surface-level* behaviors and structures.

Worldview is *the unconscious, deep-level assumptions people have about reality as they perceive it; assumptions about how the world works and how to relate to and interact with all the things, events and people encountered in life* (Rogers 2002:27).

As children, we learn our worldview as we grow—in our specific social and cultural contexts. The word *absorb* may be a more descriptive way of describing the process than the word learn. We do not learn our worldview the way we learn the multiplication tables. No one sits us down to teach us worldview. For the most part, worldview is *transmitted* to us informally and unintentionally within our cultural context as we listen to and observe our parents or other significant people in our lives. As we listen, observe, and experience we learn and form impressions about living life in our cultural context. The impressions we form become assumptions about life. We do not question these assumptions. We simply accept them.

Our level-one worldview assumptions are the basis for our level-two internal responses (values, feelings, thinking), which are the basis for our level-three cultural structures and behaviors. The kind of funerals we have, for instance, and the way we act at funerals, traces its way back down the chain to our worldview assumptions about life and death. As Hiebert has noted, worldview is not what we think about, but *what we think with*. Our worldview assumptions guide us in how we think about life.

In the next section we will explore the historical circumstance and events that worked to shape Western culture. As we begin to understand how Western culture evolved we will begin to get a feel for why Americans are they way the are.

Part 2

Western Culture

Chapter 2

The Development of Ancient Israel
and the
Jewish Religion

To understand 21st century Western culture requires that we examine some specific events that occurred approximately 4,000 years ago (about 2,000 BC). In the ancient Mesopotamian city of Ur, a man named Abram received a message from God that set in motion a chain of events that have had more impact on human history than any other events or series of events in history.

To set up this part of the history so that it makes sense it is necessary that I provide some theological as well as historical background. The history and theology are entwined in such a way that neither makes much sense without the other.

God's Plan for Humankind

God had a goal that he wanted to accomplish. Humans had sinned and ruined their relationship with him. He wanted a way to restore his relationship with humankind so he devised a plan to that end. His plan involved becoming a human being himself and offering himself as a sacrifice for the sins of humanity so people could be forgiven and saved in spite of their evil behavior.

God decided that the best way to accomplish his goal of becoming a human being was to have a special group of people who lived according to a strict code of behavior that involved the recognition of the one true God, of moral absolutes, of personal responsibility, of sin and its consequences, of spiritual values and ethical standards, of goodness and love and a relationship with God. When this group of people, a cultural group unlike any other, was sufficiently developed and established and regional sociopolitical conditions were right, God, through an amazing miraculous process, would be born into that group of people, becoming a human being so he could carry out his plan of reconciliation.

Interesting plan. But where would God get a group of people that met his standards? There were no cultural groups like the one he envisioned. He would have to create one. To do that, God decided to start with a man he knew, a man named Abram. Abram's family was from Ur, a city of ancient Mesopotamia (modern day Iraq). His father, Terah, decided to move his family to Canaan, which lay to the East, across the Arabian Desert. Caravans did not cross the desert, but followed a northerly route known as the Fertile Crescent which eventually circled down into Canaan. It was a long, difficult, exhausting journey. When they got to the city of Haran, about half way to Canaan, Tarah decided to settle his family there.

Abram, who was in his seventies at the time and married to Sarai, continued to live with his father in Haran until Terah died. God then told Abram to leave Haran and go to the place where God would lead him. God made three promises to Abram. God told Abram 1) that Abram would be the father of a great nation of people, 2) that he (God) would bless Abram, make him famous, and make him a blessing to other people, and 3) that he would also bless other people who were good to Abram but would not bless those who were not good to Abram. Abram believed God and set out on the journey with God as his guide.

Canaan was the destination and the new nation of people God would create to accomplish his purposes would be Abram's descendents, the people known as Israel. The story is rather long and involved and if you have read the Bible or seen many biblical movies you probably know at least some of the story. Abram's name was changed to Abraham. He had a son named Isaac, who had a son named Jacob, who had twelve sons, one of whom was Joseph. Joseph's brothers were jealous of him and sold him into slavery. Joseph ended up in Egypt, impressed the Pharaoh with his abilities, and eventually became the second most powerful man in the world at that time.

A famine hit that part of the world and there was no food anywhere, except in Egypt. God, of course had arranged all that and Jacob's family back in Canaan had to go to Egypt to buy grain for food. Jacob sent his sons to Egypt who ended up having to deal with their brother whom they had sold into slavery. It was all very dramatic and Joseph ended up forgiving his brothers and Jacob was reunited with his long lost son when the whole family moved to Egypt to live in comfort and security.

Politics in Egypt changed, however, and Joseph's family, who had grown into a very substantial group of people, were forced into slavery. Four hundred years later the slave nation of Israel had grown into a few million people and God decided it was time to move his plan into the next phase. God raised up Moses to deliver his people from Egyptian slavery. God wanted his people to leave Egypt. Pharaoh didn't want to lose his source of free labor. After confrontations and plagues and all sorts of intrigue and drama, including a lot of people dying, Pharaoh told Moses the Israelites could leave Egypt.

God's Special Agreement with Israel

Three months later the Israelites arrived at the foot of Mount Sinai where God offered to enter into a special agreement with them. The offer was simple: they would be his special people whom he would care for and bless if they agreed to live by his rules. If they would worship him and only him and obey his rules, he would take care of them. Life would be good.

God's offer sounded like a good deal so the Israelites agreed. Sometime around 1,446 BC, Moses climbed Mount Sinai and God gave him the Ten Commandments, which were the foundation of the formal agreement between God and the Israelites. These laws were known as the Law of Moses. When everything in the agreement was spelled out, there were approximately 613 laws, but the Ten Commandments provided the foundational concepts of the agreement. Read them over and you will get an idea of how God expected his people to live.

> *I am the LORD your God, who rescued you from slavery in Egypt.*
> *Do not worship any other gods besides me.*
> *Do not make idols of any kind, whether in the shape of birds or animals or fish. You must never worship or bow down to them, for I, the LORD your God, am a jealous God who will not share your affection with any other god! I do not leave unpunished the sins of those who hate me, but I punish the children for the sins of their parents to the third and fourth generations. But I lavish my love on those who love me and obey my commands, even for a thousand generations.*
> *Do not misuse the name of the LORD your God. The LORD will not let you go unpunished if you misuse his name.*
> *Remember to observe the Sabbath day by keeping it holy. Six days a week are set apart for your daily duties and regular work, but the seventh day is a day of rest dedicated to the LORD your God. On that day no one in your household may do any kind of work. This includes you, your sons and daughters, your male and female servants, your livestock, and any foreigners living among you. For in six days the LORD made*

the heavens, the earth, the sea, and everything in them; then he
rested on the seventh day. That is why the LORD blessed the
Sabbath day and set it apart as holy.

Honor your father and mother. Then you will live a long,
full life in the land the LORD your God will give you.

Do not murder.

Do not commit adultery.

Do not steal.

Do not testify falsely against your neighbor.

Do not covet your neighbor's house. Do not covet your
neighbor's wife, male or female servant, ox or donkey, or
anything else your neighbor owns, (Exodus 20:2-17).

These Ten Commandments, along with the other 603 laws of the agreement between God and Israel, guided the development of Israel's society as they eventually settled in Canaan and became the nation God would use as his vehicle for entry into the world. The culture of Israel developed as it did largely because of the requirements of their agreement with God. While they did not live up to the terms of the agreement as they should have, and while God had to discipline them many times (as a father disciplines unruly children), Israel's culture was quite different than those of other nations at that time.

A Unique Culture in the Ancient World

The social structure that evolved in Israel (because of the nature of the special agreement between God and the Israelites) was unique in the ancient world. They were monotheistic with the highest moral standards humans had ever known. God's laws constituted moral absolutes. Right was right and wrong was wrong and that was that. An awareness of sin was a social reality because the people seemed unable to discipline themselves to live as God expected. They broke God's laws—often. Along with the presence of sin came the possibility of forgiveness, based on repentance. The people were to avoid disobedience and strive for moral uprightness, that is, for personal growth into the image and likeness of God. God explained to his people, *because I am holy you must be holy.* They belonged to God and were his representative in the world. It was necessary then, that their ways of living reflect his values, his nature. This was why their culture was to be different.

The agreement between God and Israel included laws regarding personal holiness, social responsibility (caring for the poor, for instance), and acknowledging the goodness and presence of God in one's life by engaging in corporate worship and giving a portion of one's income back to God by means of a required donation to the priesthood. The income was a blessing from God in the first place, so giving a percentage (ten percent) back to him was appropriate.

The Israelites, who became known as Jews, often fell into very sinful ways of thinking and living. For this they had to be punished by God. But eventually they became very serious about holiness. They were determined to be different than the nations around them that were polytheistic and immoral.

Eventually God decided it was time to carry out his plan to become human. So during the days of the Roman Empire, when Augustus was Emperor, Mary became pregnant by the power of the Holy Spirit and God became a human being in the person of Jesus. The presence of Jesus was the fulfillment of all the promises God had made to the Israelites. Through Jesus' ministry and the subsequent ministries of the men Jesus trained to carry on his work after his return to heaven, God took things in a very different direction. We will discuss that different direction in Chapter 4 when we discuss Christianity. For now the point is that the foundational concepts of Judaism were carried over into Christian thought and practice and influenced a great deal of Western thought and practice.

Ancient Judaism's Impact on Western Culture

The fundamental concepts of Judaism became foundational concepts of the Christian system. If you think of Christianity as a tree, with a strong trunk and branches that reach far out in all directions, the roots of that gigantic tree are Jewish. Christianity, which grew up out of Judaism, impacted Rome and ultimately the West so thoroughly, that concepts that were originally Jewish had a considerable impact on Western culture. Judeo-Christian traditions were part of Western culture and were spread as Western culture spread.

Monotheism

The most obvious of Judaism's influence on the West is perhaps its monotheism. The Jews believed not just in the concept of God, but in one eternal creator God who had revealed himself to them, selecting them as his representatives. The idea of the one and only eternal God who has specifically and precisely revealed himself through the Hebrew Scriptures (and subsequently the Christian Scriptures as well), providing humankind with a framework for acceptable and successful living has been a hallmark of Western civilization since the fourth century when the Roman Emperor Constantine adopted Christianity as the official religion of the Roman Empire.

By divine design, Christianity became to the world what Judaism had been to the Israelites. If the Israelites had been God's chosen people. By extension, Christians became God's special people, commissioned to span the globe with the message of reconciliation and relationship with the one God through faith in Jesus.

Though there have always been unbelievers in the West, their numbers have been relatively small. The West has been and remains a monotheistic culture.

35

Moral Absolutes

Until recently, nearly everyone in Western culture believed in moral absolutes. In Chapter 9 I'll explain why some no longer do. For the moment, however, let us consider what has been true in the West for nearly 2,000 years. Belief in the existence of moral absolutes (provided by God) gave Western culture with a set of foundational beliefs that clearly defined the boundaries of right and wrong. While everyone understood that there were gray areas that required special consideration, there were a set of moral absolutes that were firmly in place at the foundation of Western culture. For most Western people, these absolutes would have included but not been limited to the Ten Commandments. Lying in general, not just false witness, was considered wrong. Sexual immorality in general (including homosexuality), not just adultery, was considered wrong. Intoxication, regardless of which drug induced it, was considered morally wrong.

On and on the list could go, but the point is that Western people (especially Americans) believed in a set of divinely ordained moral absolutes that were simply beyond debate. When God said a behavior was unacceptable it was unacceptable. Thus, until just recently, social expectations for proper behavior were narrower than is presently the case.

Such moral absolutes can be traced in a direct line all the way back to the Judaism of ancient Israel.

A Guilt-Justice Orientation

Some cultures, many Asian and African cultures for instance, are shame-honor cultures rather than guilt-justice cultures. Social control in shame-honor societies is rooted in avoiding behavior that will bring shame on oneself or one's family and on behaving in ways that will bring honor to oneself and one's family. The West, however, is a guilt-justice culture. The focus in a guilt-justice culture is on avoiding behavior that violates laws and results in guilt. Social control is maintained by negative consequences (justice) being carried out if one is found to be guilty of breaking laws or rules.

The focus in guilt-justice cultures is on avoiding wrong things and doing right things because wrong is wrong and right is right. But justice in a guilt-justice culture is not only associated with punishment, but also with fair treatment for everyone—justice for all—because that is what is right and fair. A guilt-justice orientation is rooted in the idea of moral absolutes, sin, personal responsibility, and all people being equal under the law, entitled to fair and just treatment—at least theoretically. These were fundamental themes in ancient Israel and the Jewish social system, growing out of the idea that God is a just God (Forrester 2000:360). God's people, therefore, must be people of justice.

Lower Courts and Higher Courts Rendering Judgments Based on the Rule of Law

After the Israelites left Egypt and were on their way to Mount Sinai, Moses, upon the advice of his father-in-law, Jethro, set up what we would call a court system that involved lower courts and higher courts. Moses had been hearing all the cases and disputes that occurred among the people. The case load was exhausting and he was not being effective as a leader because he was stretched too thin. His father-in-law advised him to appoint men to serve as judges over groups of people: groups of 10, 50, 100, and 1,000. Only the most difficult cases would be brought to Moses for a decision. Moses took Jethro's advice and established a court system which became the basis for judicial structure in many places.

A key concept in the system had to do with the rule of law rather than the whims of the judges. A code of law that transcends the interests of individual rulers is foundational to the idea of justice for all. Israel's Law of Moses was not the first written law code. Ancient Mesopotamian texts predate it. However, they are not as extensive, nor has their impact been felt for centuries throughout the Western world as has the code of ancient Israel. The laws given to Moses by God and the system of judicial management put into place by Moses continues to impact the West even today.

Summary

Ancient Israel came into existence as a result of God's direct activity and intervention in human history. God specifically created a nation of people though whom he worked to accomplish his specific purpose—saving humans from the consequences of own foolish sinful behavior. God wanted/needed a group of people that would live differently than humans were living. He wanted a society of people whose values and behavior reflected something beyond the needs and impulses of physical existence. God wanted a people whose culture reflected his own holiness, goodness, and justice.

To have such a group of people necessitated not only that God create a new nation of people, but also that he provide them with a code of conduct designed to create an atmosphere and framework for daily living that reflected his values and expectations for how people ought to live. The code of conduct he gave them is known as the Law of Moses. It contained approximately 613 laws that became the foundation for the development of a culture that was unlike any that had existed.

What Judaism was intended to be for the Israelites, Christianity was intended to be for all people. Christianity was the tree that grew up out of the roots of Judaism. Because many of the foundational concepts of Judaism were absorbed into Christian theology, those Jewish ideas and practices were passed on to the West as Judeo-Christian traditions, and were spread along with Western culture.

The major Jewish traditions that continue to impact Western culture today, at least to a degree, are monotheism, belief in moral absolutes, a guilt-justice orientation, and a judicial system of lower courts and higher courts rendering judgments based on the rule of law rather than the impulses of rulers.

These are not by any means the only influences that have shaped Western culture and not all Western people have embraced all of these concepts. However, that some of the beliefs and practices of ancient Israel have shaped Western culture is beyond dispute.

In the next chapter we will examine the role of Greek philosophy and science on Western culture.

Chapter 3

The Development of
Greek Culture, Philosophy, and Science

The Law of Moses and Israelite culture was nearly 1,000 years old before Greece emerged from her years of cultural darkness and during her golden age began exhibiting the traits that have been celebrated throughout the ages. Before thinking specifically about the ways Greek culture has impacted Western culture, it might be helpful to review some basic history.

Background and Overview[3]

Before the Greeks began building their civilization, the Minoan civilization of Crete dominated the islands and the lands surrounding the Aegean Sea. Their presence was felt from 1600 to 1400 BC. During the same time the people of Mycenae (on the Greek mainland) built a rich civilization that flourished until 1200 BC. The Mycenaeans were a

---

[3] This historical background material was originally published in another of my books: *The Bible Culturally Speaking: The Role of Culture in the Production, Presentation and Interpretation of God's Word*, published by Mission and Ministry Resources, copyright 2004.

wealthy people who delighted in building. Some of their palaces had walls ten feet thick. They were an industrious people with a highly evolved society. Records discovered by archeologists indicate a royal bureaucracy that included "tax assessments, land holdings, agricultural stores, and inventories of slaves, horses, and chariot parts." They list over 100 occupations present in Mycenaean society, including: goldsmiths, shipwrights, masons, bakers, cooks, woodcutters, messengers, longshoremen, oarsmen, saddlers, shepherds, dry cleaners, doctors, heralds, potters, foresters, carpenters, bowmakers, weavers, bath attendants, and unguent boilers" (Bowra 1965:32). They were also a warrior society.

Over a period of years the Mycenaean society gradually disintegrated. Civil strife, economic disruption, and successive waves of invasion and infiltration by a group of people from the North called the Dorians, proved to be more than the Mycenaean civilization could withstand. The Dorians became a formidable presence in Greece (on the mainland and throughout the Islands), though they were not able to subjugate all of the native Greeks. Athens, for instance, was able to stand against their invasion (33-34).

The fall of the Mycenaean civilization plunged Greece into 450 years of social darkness. From 1200 to 750 BC, "the Greek world passed through a Dark Age from which only scattered legends and unrewarding artifacts survive" (32). But when that Dark Age past, the Greeks began to define themselves more clearly (Starr 1991:205). The City-State evolved and the political, social, and philosophical foundations that made Greece great were laid.

Greek City-states were originally ruled by kings. Each city (*polis*) was an independent entity. But those independent, local kings were gradually replaced in each polis by a counsel of aristocrats—wealthy Greeks who thought themselves superior to those not of their own socioeconomic class. The citizens of a polis would assemble periodically to elect officials and vote on issues (208). Bowra notes that Greek citizens assembled 40 times each year to deliberate on important issues (1965:108). Greek society was not egalitarian, but all citizens, regardless of social standing, were protected by law and enjoyed justice.

The splendor of Greek society—their beautiful works of art, their political and philosophical contributions—have been the focus of much attention for centuries. Yet the mundane permeated their society as well. Freeman has noted that "the majority of Greeks spent most of their time as farmers. . . 90 percent of the population of ancient Greece cultivated the land and had no other option if their city was to survive" (1996:169).

Two factors beyond their control made their agricultural endeavors a backbreaking task to be endured: poor soil conditions and unpredictable rainfall. Primitive tools did not make the job any easier, and the ever-present possibility of insufficient rainfall, resulting in a poor crop, lent itself to a constant anxiety. Maintaining a surplus of grain and other produce was essential for survival in drought years as well as for trade and dowries for daughters.

Planting and harvesting were busy times. During slack times, after planting in early spring and during the summer and early fall before harvest, the Greeks would busy themselves with their athletic games (170).

As is always the case, the Greek agricultural economy involved caring for animals. Sheep and goats required pasture. Shepherds would move herds across the lands outside the polis. No one owned the land. Herds were moved from place to place depending on grazing and water (171).

Even though farming provided the foundation of Greek society, there was a manufacturing aspect as well. Sheep were sheared for wool; iron, and clay were mined and sold. These enterprises were small scale, but contributed in a meaningful way to the economy (171).

Though the Greeks have become renowned for their advanced thinking in some areas (democracy, the rule of law, philosophy, the importance of the individual), in other areas their thinking was limited (as it is for all people) by their worldview and cultural assumptions. Their thinking regarding slavery was one of these areas. It is estimated that in 430 BC the population of Attica, a polis not far from Athens, was 315,000. About 115,000 (over 36 percent) of them were slaves (Bowra 1965:94).

The most common form of slavery was "chattel" slavery. The slave was owned outright by his or her master and had no rights whatsoever. Slaves worked in the mines, on farms, in workshops, or in households in various capacities. Household slaves might be involved in cleaning and cooking and other household chores. Some household slaves served as teachers or household overseers. Their daily lives may have been quite comfortable compared to those who worked in other capacities.

Not all Greeks advocated slavery. Bowra points out that the playwright Euripides referred to slavery as evil by its very nature, for it required a kind of submission that was beyond that which should be expected of anyone. Aristotle, however, attempted to defend slavery by suggesting that some people were naturally inclined to servitude (1965:95).

Another aspect of Greek society where otherwise enlightened people seemed to be operating in the dark had to do with the place of women in society. Greek society was patriarchal to the extreme. Greek boys were educated. Greek girls were not. Greek men were required to be involved in society. Greek women were not permitted to be involved in matters outside the home to any significant degree. In the older ages of Greek society women enjoyed greater freedom, though were never allowed to engage in politics. As centuries passed, however, their freedoms were limited. Their place was in the home and their role in society was to have children and to keep silent (95). Property was owned by men and inheritance was patrilineal. In families where there were no sons to inherit, the daughter who inherited would be married to a near kinsman (effectively allowing him to inherit) so property would remain in the family.

The city of Sparta appears to have provided an exception in these matters. Sparta had been dominated by Dorian attitudes and was more interested in warfare than other Greek cities. The men of Sparta were often away on military campaigns leaving their wives to manage affairs on the home front, thus allowing them greater social and economic latitude.

The most important day in a woman's life was her wedding day. Greek women (girls) would be married between the ages of ten and fifteen to husbands in their late twenties or early thirties. A young woman would go directly from her father's house to her husband's. Marriages were arranged. Dowries were paid. And while it is not entirely accurate to say that women in ancient Greece were thought of as property, for all practical purposes that is the way life was lived (Freeman 1996:177-178).

The wedding ceremony consisted of a purifying bath for the bride followed by a ride with the groom and his best friend in a cart to the groom's house. Upon arriving at the groom's home the new wife would be welcomed to the family by her mother-in-law before being taken to the bedroom where she and her husband would consummate the marriage (178).

Religion in ancient Greece was polytheistic. "The aim of Greek cult [religion] was to protect mankind during its life and to secure continuation of the group. Problems of individual survival after death, of individual ethics, or even of the origins of the world emerged only partially and were not always to be answered in religious terms" (Starr 1991:238). Religious rituals and sacrifices were conducted at the altars outside of local temples. Prayers to the various deities were offered inside the temple. Twelve gods or goddesses were eventually elevated to primary positions— the gods of Mount Olympus. Zeus was the father, Hera was his wife, Poseidon, Hestia, and Demeter were his brothers and sisters. Zeus' children were Athena, Artemis, Aphrodite, Apollo, Hermes, Ares, and Hephaestus. In addition to these primary gods and goddesses there were numerous other local deities worshipped throughout the Greek world.

It was to these gods and goddesses, and other powerful supernatural creatures, that the Greeks prayed and offered sacrifices in order to assure a plentiful harvest, safe passage during travels, profitable business, victory in battle, and whatever else may have been perceived to be in the hands of the gods. Prayer, of course, was an important element in Greek worship. The central feature, however, was an animal sacrifice offered by the family father on their behalf. The animal (usually a sheep or goat) was slaughtered and bled. The blood, along with the fat around internal organs would be burnt in sacrifice. The meat of the animal would be cooked and consumed in a ritual meal by the family offering the sacrifice. If all of the meat could not be consumed it would be sold in the marketplace.

One of the reasons Greek culture became such a dominant force in the ancient world was that in spite of some of its shortcomings it was an excellent civilization. They did things well. The other reason was Alexander the Great. The Greek City-states eventually came under the control of Philip of Macedonia. When Philip died in 336 BC, his son, Alexander, at the age of 20, became king in his father's place. Bowra notes that:

> [W]hen Alexander ascended the throne at the age of 20, Macedonia's power was so firmly established, and Philip's policy of expansion so well developed, that the young king with his dream of a unified world needed only to pick up where his father had left off, (1965:157).

Alexander set out to consolidate his control of Greece and did so without too much difficulty. Only Sparta successfully resisted Alexander's dominance. Rather than engage in a protracted war with the powerful Spartans, Alexander allowed them to remain independent.

Once Alexander had solidified his control over nearby regions, he set his sights on the Persian Empire. The Persian Empire was gradually weakening, and since 401 BC the Greeks had known they could defeat the Persians. A Persian renegade named Cyrus had been determined to take the throne of his brother Artaxerxes II. He hired an army of Greek mercenaries as his invading force. Cyrus was killed and the Greek army was held off but not defeated. In fact, they defeated the left wing of the Persian forces and were able to make their way safely back home through Persian territory. Because of that victory, Alexander knew he could defeat the Persians. He began his campaign.

Aristotle had been Alexander's teacher. He instilled in Alexander a love for all things Greek. As Alexander began his push south and east his plan was to civilize the world by establishing a Greek empire. In each region his army conquered, Alexander established Greek cities. Soldiers were allowed to settle and become residents, marrying local women and establishing Greek culture (Freeman 1996:273).

Spreading Greek culture was one of Alexander's goals. He wanted to unite East and West in one grand culture that was Greek through and through. That meant speaking the Greek language, understanding Greek philosophy, attending the theater and stripping naked to exercise at the gymnasium. It meant thinking and acting like a civilized Greek in every respect. Alexander, however, and those who came after him, were wise enough to allow for cultural variation due to local and religious traditions. Jews, for instance, were not going to strip naked and exercise at the gymnasium, and they were going to continue the practice of circumcision—a practice considered barbaric by the Greeks. Generally speaking, however, Alexander accomplished his goal. The known world at that time, so Greek in its outlook, was truly a *Hellenized* world (Freeman 1996:274-283).

The Greek Legacy

In *The Greek Achievement*, Charles Freeman has said:

> The Greeks provided the chromosomes of Western civilization. . . Greek ways of exploring the *cosmos*, defining the problem of knowledge (and what is meant by knowledge itself) creating the language in which such problems are explored, representing the physical world and human society in the arts, defining the nature of value, describing the past, still underlie the Western cultural tradition. In some areas, the creation of mathematics, for instance, the legacy has become a universal one. All mathematicians everywhere work within the framework whose foundations are Greek, (1999:434).

In a similar vein, Bruce Thornton has noted:

> [I]t was the Greeks who first began to recognize a common humanity more important than local or tribal affiliations. It was the Greek Diogenes who identified himself as a "citizen of the world" rather than just a member of some parochial city-state. Without that recognition of a common humanity, slavery might never have been abolished in the West, women might never have been granted equality (as they still have not in some non-Western countries), and the liberal notion of innate rights possessed by all humans merely by virtue of being human would never have existed, (2000:10).

It's not that contemporary Western culture on a day-to-day basis is very similar to the culture of the ancient Greeks. It is not. But many of the ideas that are foundational for Western culture are ideas that were born and nourished, cultivated and advanced by the Greeks. And

47

regardless of how different the fruit may look from the seed the Greeks planted, many of the seeds they planted have born fruit in the Western world. What were some of the seeds the Greeks planted?

Democracy

After a couple of false starts and stumbles, democracy took root in Athens and from 508 until 322 BC provided the world with proof that people could govern themselves.

In describing democracy in Athens during those 186 years, C. W. Blackwell notes that:

> Democracy in Athens was not limited to giving citizens the right to vote. Athens was not a republic, nor were the People governed by a representative body of legislators. In a very real sense, the People governed themselves, debating and voting individually on issues great and small, from matters of war and peace to the proper qualifications for ferry-boat captains (2003:2)

The central institution of the Athenian democracy was the Assembly, the *ekklesia*. This *Assembly of Citizens* was composed of Athenian citizens, free men over 18 years old. When a young man turned 18, he would appear before the officials of the voting district in which he lived. He had to be able to demonstrate that he was 18, that he was not a slave and that his parents were Athenians. If he was able to satisfy the officials, the young man's name was recorded on the Assembly list and he could then participate in the Assembly of Citizens (2003:3-10).

The Assembly would meet 40 times over the course of a year to listen to, discuss, and vote on issues of all sorts, important and mundane. All Assembly members could speak and express their opinion. A *herald* (an Assembly manager) would call out, "Who wishes to address the

Assembly?" The only regulation appears to have been that out of respect for citizens over 50 years old, those senior citizens were allowed to speak first. Votes were taken openly by a show of hands. Citizens were reimbursed for their time spent in government affairs, (2003:3-10).

It is important to think in terms of the underlying assumptions that drove the democracy of Athens. What assumptions about the person provided the foundation of their system? Clearly, they considered all "men" (that is, males) to be equal and capable of meaningful participation. That all citizens were allowed to address the Assembly indicates that they believed that each individual was worthy of consideration, of respect, and that he had a right to participate in (determine) decisions that impacted him and his society. In ancient Greece, the individual mattered, and self-determination was taken for granted.

While it is clear that the Greeks were advanced and liberated thinkers, it is also clear that they were not that advanced in all aspects of their thinking. Women were not considered equal to males and slavery was practiced. Like all people, the Greeks were captives (to a degree) of their time and place and sometimes, like all people, *did not see the forest for the trees.* However, their focus on individuality and self-determination, on the ability and right of citizens to govern themselves (even if their definition of a citizen was too narrow) laid a foundation for future generations of like-minded people to build upon, creating other forms of democratic self-government. And though our American "democracy" is markedly different from that of ancient Athens (Cahill 2003:14), their assumptions regarding the nature of the individual, society, and government that lay beneath their democratic forms also drive modern Western culture in our thinking about the individual, society, and government.

Philosophy and Science

Philosophy developed in ancient Greece because of their deep and sustained curiosity about the world (Oliver 1997:14). They were curious about everything so they analyzed everything. They were not bound by religious assumptions or superstitions. There were no categories of life that were beyond critical analysis. Nothing was off limits or out of bounds.

The earliest Greek philosopher/scientists were as interested in matters of science as they were matters of philosophy. Questions about *physis*, nature, included thinking about mathematics, especially geometry, as well as inquiries regarding the nature of existence or the origin of all that exists.

The earliest Greek philosophers included: *Pythagoras*, founder of the systematic study of geometry; *Thales*, who theorized that all things were made out of water; *Anaximander*, who probably prepared the first map of the world and invented the sundial; *Anaximenes*, who speculated that air, not water, was the ultimate element; and *Xenophanes*, who was likely the first philosopher of religion, was an avowed monotheist who argued that there was one great God, doing so not on theological grounds but on rational grounds (Kenny 1998:1-18). Notice how the first four were focused on mathematics and the physical sciences. For centuries philosophy and science were different sides of the same coin.

A dozen others that lived and thought in sixth century BC Greece could be highlighted, but these illustrate the presence of a widespread spirit of inquiry into the nature of the world that characterized the ancient Greeks. A lot of their ideas turned out to be wrong. But at least they were thinking and theorizing. It was their spirit of inquiry, their curious nature that demanded critical analysis, hypothesis, and theory that drove them deeper into inquiry and lifted them above the tyranny of superstition and dogma.

It was in the fifth century, however, that the philosophical activity of ancient Greece reached its pinnacle. While few may be familiar with the names of Thales, Anaximander and Xenophanes, most people educated in the West are familiar with the names of Socrates, Plato, and Aristotle.

Concerning the philosophy of fifth century Greece, Oliver has noted that:

> No other era of philosophy has had such a bearing on so much of Western society. The works of Socrates, Plato, and Aristotle have influenced modern politics, ethics, science and culture and their ideas are as hotly debated today as when they were conceived 2,400 years ago, (1997:9).

Socrates

Socrates, who said that the unexamined life is not worth living, was concerned with the meaning of virtue. For him, moral knowledge and virtue were the same. Those who know the right thing to do will do the right thing. Those who do not do the right things in life, according to Socrates, obviously do not know the right things to do.

Socrates may have been influenced by the Sophists and their concerns with how to live an excellent life. He rejected the traditional gods of Greek society and was considered a dangerous revolutionary by the political leaders of his day. He was feared because by his questions he could make them look are foolish and incompetent as perhaps they were, and because he was adored by the young Athenians who followed him (Kidd, 1967:480-485).

For all of his inquiry into morals and virtue, Socrates acknowledged that his wisdom was worth nothing. However, he was quick to add that the man who acknowledges that he knows nothing is wiser than those who do not (Kenny 1998:24).

Plato

Plato was born in 427 BC and was a student of Socrates. Concerning Plato, Oliver suggests that "there has not been another philosopher singularly more influential than Plato. . . his writings are important not only as great works of philosophy, but also as the founding documents of Western culture," (1997:18). Oliver also alludes to the fact that many philosophers suggest that philosophy, as we think of it, actually began with Plato.

- In 387 Plato established a school, known as the *Academy*, for the training of politicians. Over the years Plato produced an impressive body of work. *Republic* is his most significant writing. It has to do with the nature of justice, politics, and epistemology (the theory of knowledge). In *Symposium*, Plato deals with the nature of love; in *Meno* he takes up a discussion of virtue and knowledge and the relationship between them; in *Parmenides*, he offers a critique of his own theory of forms; and in *Theaetetus* he explores knowledge and wisdom (Stangroom and Garvey 2005:13).

One of Plato's most intriguing insights is put forth in *Republic*. There, Socrates, as the main character or spokesman, tells a story about prisoners in a cave and how their perceptions are but shadows of reality that do not reflect true reality. His point (referred to as the two-world theory) is that there is the world that really is, and there is the world of human perception. The world of human perception is not an accurate reflection of the world as it really is. How, then, can humans be sure of anything? Plato's answer is that sense perception is only one source of knowledge. Intellect is another. Intellect helps clarify perception, (Hollis

1985:57-62). The trick is to learn how to use one's intellect properly.

Plato wrote about views of reality that still impact Western thought today. He wrote about the natural sciences. He wrote about what constitutes knowledge, about how rulers should be prepared to rules and how they should rule. He wrote about justice, happiness, morals and ethics, politics and law (Ryle 1967:314-333). In his own work and the work of the students he influenced and philosophers who came after him, Plato has impacted the West more, perhaps, than any other single philosopher.

Aristotle

If one were to argue that there is another philosopher whose influence outshines that of Plato, it would be Aristotle. Aristotle was born in 384 BC in Stagira in Macedonia. At 17 he went to Athens to study with Plato at the Academy. He remained there for 20 years and became one of the teachers. When Plato died, Aristotle left Athens for Macedonia, where he became the private tutor for the young Alexander (The Great).

When Alexander assumed the throne of his father Philip and began his conquests, Aristotle returned to Athens where he opened his own school in the Lyceum[4] just outside the city limits (Wedin 1999:44-51).

"Aristotle's writings were of unparalleled size and range, and out of a huge number of treatises forty-seven have survived," (Grant 1991:98). His major works are: *Nicomachean Ethics*, having to do with morality; *Politics*, having to do with the ideal state; and *Physics*, having to do with Aristotle's perception of science, space, and time

---

[4] The Lyceum was an athletic facility just outside of Athens, near a sanctuary of the god Apollo. There, Aristotle and other philosophy teachers would walk under the porticos as they lectured. Students would follow them around as they listened.

(Strangroom and Garvey 2005:18). His work in logic shaped Western thinking as much as any other single work, perhaps more; as did his answer to the question, "what is being?" (Kerferd 1967:151-162).

Aristotle was both scientist and philosopher in the truest sense of each word as it is used today. As with other ancient scientists, some of his theories have proven incorrect, but he was thoroughgoing in his investigations and inexhaustible in his inquiries. His system of logic and semantic structure is still in use today. In our section on the Middle Ages we will notice how the "discovery" of Aristotle's work some 1,400 years after his death may have made the Renaissance possible.

History

What is the difference between writing a story, relating legend, and recording history? The Greeks applied their appreciation for detail and critical analysis not only to the accurate recording of events, but to the analysis of the trustworthiness and dependability of the information. Hecataeus, who lived and wrote around 500 BC, in the preface one of his writings said, "I am here writing what to me appears to be true: for the tales of the Greeks are diverse and in my opinion, ridiculous," (Thornton 2000:151).

A storyteller tells a story, often passing on information he has been given without any kind of analysis. A historian gathers information from as many sources as possible, weighs and analyzes the data, separates fact from fiction as best he can, reports what he believes is true, and may or may not provide a personal perspective or commentary on the events.

Freeman discusses Herodotus in this light, calling him the *father of history.* Herodotus' recording of the Persian Wars, Freeman notes, "are remarkable not only for their scope but as the first recognizably "modern" work of history," (1999:185). Thornton discusses Thucydides in this same light, noting that, "Thucydides most explicitly set out a historical method predicated on the rational evaluation of evidence rather than on the fancies of myth and legend," (2000:152). This allowed for history to be "liberated from traditional tales and legends, and moved beyond the mere chronicling of events; truth was argued on the basis of a rational analysis of evidence, including the individual's own observation and experience," (151).

What prompted the Greeks to engage in such critical analysis of events? It can be traced to their belief that the world is a rational, orderly place that must be observed, analyzed and understood by rational, orderly people. Simple, shallow observations rooted in animistic supernaturalism and ignorant superstition, were simply unacceptable. A rational orderly world required rational, orderly minds to analyze, evaluate and offer rational, orderly explanations. These underlying assumptions about the nature of the world and of human beings impacted the way the Greeks interpreted and reported events. Their deep-level worldview assumptions acting as an interpretive filter, impacted how they thought about, evaluated, and recoded events.

Those same underlying assumptions have driven the way modern Western historians have analyzed and interpreted events—rational, orderly minds observing a rational, orderly world, arriving at rational, orderly conclusions.

Drama

The Greek drama traces its roots to the religious festivals designed to honor the god Dionysus. Those early festivals probably include songs and dance that, over time, evolved into plays that addressed significant political and cultural issues, thus meeting important psychological needs

(Freeman 1999:241). Theater became a crucial part of Greek culture. It was part of the Greek education.

Greek dramas were expressed either as tragedy or comedy. Tragedy had to do with the experiences of powerful people or beings (gods, heroes, kings) who encountered adversity and suffered life-changing consequences. Comedy had to do with ordinary people who encountered life's circumstances and emerged the better for it. Tragedies did not always end tragically and comedies weren't always funny.

"Tragedies," Bowra notes, "examined the nature of evil in an effort to edify the mind by showing how great and heroic spirits behaved in the presence of evil," (1965:145). They were intended to help people in their struggle to find meaning in life, to understand suffering, to develop means for effective coping. Are people subject to the whims of fate beyond their control? Will the people's own weaknesses be insurmountable and lead to failure? Even if the dramas could not provide satisfactory answers, there was benefit in having acknowledged and wrestled with the issues involved, (Freeman 1999:243).

In typical Greek fashion, Aristotle analyzed the drama and concluded that there were six things necessary for the tragedy to be effective[5]:

1. plot: a unified story with a beginning, middle and end; simple but compelling,
2. character: the main character must not be too good or too bad, someone with whom the audience can identify,
3. diction: what the characters say must be interesting, compelling, and "in character,"
4. thought: what they think must also be in character, and compelling,

---

[5] The list of items is Aristotle's as listed by Kenny 1998:61, the definitions of each item are my own.

5. spectacle: visually compelling,
6. melody: music must carry the mood of the story.

If one studies playwriting of screenwriting today, these same features are considered essential for success.

Greek drama was lost for a period of time, but rediscovered in the 1,600s. Today, Greek dramas are presented on college campuses and in theaters across the country. Even more important, however, than their reproduction on the stage, is the impact the Greek drama has had on Western storytelling in general. Analyze any good movie or movie series, such as *Lord of the Rings*, *Matrix*, *Star Wars*, or a dozen others, and you will find all the elements Aristotle identified. The elements of Greek drama are fundamental in telling a good story, in getting the audience involved, in asking and struggling with the important and challenging issues of life.

Because of the influence of the Greeks, Western storytellers (novelists, playwrites, screenwriters and directors) are the best in the world. From *Titanic*, to *Superman*, to *The Chronicles of Narnia*, to *Harry Potter*, the Greek tragedy and comedy are still with us—in different forms, yes—but still asking the same questions, making the same observations, helping us wrestle with the same challenging questions of life in an uncertain world.

Warfare Strategy

Though modern Western warfare bears little resemblance to ancient Greek warfare, the underlying beliefs that drive the machinery of modern warfare are rooted in ancient Greek perspective and purposes.

The *hoplite* warrior as part of a fighting machine was the basic component of the Greek army. The name hoplite comes from the name of the shield they carried, a *hoplon*, a large, heavy shield carried on the left arm. In their right

57

hand the hoplite carried a nine-foot spear that would be thrust out ahead of them. They also carried a short, straight iron sword for closer work. Full battle dress for a hoplite— helmet, breastplate, sword, spear, graves—weighed approximately 65 pounds (Freeman 1999:116-117; Grant 1991:10).

Troops would line up shoulder to shoulder, hidden behind brightly and fiercely decorated shields, with spears at ready. They moved as one in a powerful, coordinated unstoppable assault force. Their presence and approach was designed to strike terror in the hearts of the enemy. In their unity, strength, and precision they became a devastating killing machine capable of defeating an enemy with a considerably larger force, which they did more than once.

The Greeks were well aware of the brutality of war and the suffering it brings, yet of its necessity and appropriateness in matters of geopolitical acquisition, security, and even religious concerns (Thornton 2000: 92-100).

What made the Greek war machine so effective? Grant (1991:10) and Cahill (2003:45) both allude to the corporate mentality of the Greek army. Hoplite soldiers were not individuals fighting together, they were a corporate fighting machine that moved and fought as a single, powerful, unified entity who struck fear in the heart of the enemy.

But their presence, unity and power were not the only factors involved in their success. Cahill observes:

> [T]he Greek army can be spotted—amid all the expressions of heroism—as the brutal innovation it actually was: a mass of men no longer individuals but subject to an iron discipline, technologically superior to their opponents, their generals having learned that wars must be managed artfully, each battle planned and played out in the mind before the armies are engaged, and that, insofar as possible, the time, the place and the conditions of battle are to be chosen beforehand to enhance one's own position and put the enemy at a disadvantage. From

this moment in the late eighth century [BC], the Western war machine is operational, its objective to field a force so lethal as to inspire abject terror in all opponents; and Western soldiers march through history no longer exemplars of aristocratic valor but as the component parts they actually are, (2003:45).

The Greeks understood the importance of war management. Planning was crucial to execution. They also understood the emotional element. One of their tactics was to terrorize before overpowering. The phraseology used by the United States in recent Middle Eastern conflicts comes to mind—*shock and awe*.

Though modern Western warfare is radically different in form from that of the ancient Greeks, the underlying assumptions about effective warfare that gave the Greeks an advantage remain factors in modern Western conflict strategy.

Greek Culture and Greek Worldview

The democracy, the philosophy, the drama and literature, their ways of investigating, analyzing, critiquing, reporting, their ways of managing life and its conflicts, all the things that made Greek culture what it was, grew out of the Greek worldview.

As we saw in Chapter 1, surface-level cultural structures and behaviors grow out of mid-level internal values, feelings and thinking. These mid-level internal aspects of a people grow out of their deep-level worldview assumptions. How a people act depends on how they think and feel about things, and on their values. How they think and feel, and what is important to them depends on their assumptions about reality and about how life is to be lived. A people's surface-level culture reveals a great deal about their underlying worldview assumptions.

The way the Greeks lived tells us a great deal about their worldview. They believed the world was a rational, orderly place that could be studied and understood, so they studied it, naturalistically rather than supernaturalistically—even though they were very religious. They believed in the value and inherent worth of the individual, so as a group of individuals they governed themselves and pursued life on their own terms.

We could dig deeper, but these two assumptions alone allow for significant reflection. Greek assumptions about the nature of the world and the nature of the person provided a significant portion of the foundation upon which their culture was built. Indeed, all of Western culture is rooted in similar assumptions regarding the nature of the world and of the individual. The Greeks led the way and the West has followed.

The Greeks: Absorbed, Lost and Rediscovered

Because the Greeks were so stubbornly independent they failed to form the kind of coalition that could have resisted Rome's advances. But they did not. Alexander's kingdom, after his death, was divided up among his generals and weakened in the process. Rome was powerful and on the rise while Greece was in decline. It was, perhaps, inevitable that the Greek civilization be absorbed into the powerful and rapidly expanding Roman Empire (Grant 1991:133).

Much of what Rome had to offer was Greek in origin. Roman gods were Greek gods with Latin names. Greek philosophy was imported to Rome, as was Greek drama. So was the Greek language. Imperial business may have been conducted in Latin, but the everyday language of the Roman Empire was Greek. The geopolitical entity known as the Greek Empire may have disintegrated, but Greek civilization did not. Alexander had Hellenized the known world. The light of Greek culture was not to be extinguished—for a while.

But the light of Greek culture did eventually fade away. As the Roman Empire collapsed under the weight of internal degeneration—moral decay, high taxes, inflation, public health issues, corruption, military spending, and more—and Barbarian invasion from without, the darkness of an ignorant, uncivilized time spread over the Western world. The enlightened mind of Greek inquiry, analysis, philosophy and science, gave way to the ignorant, brutish, superstitious mind of the Dark Ages.

Fortunately the human mind can only stumble in darkness for so long before it seeks the light once again. In the Late Middle Ages, "scholars" rediscovered Greek philosophy. The works of Aristotle and others were translated and made available and the Greeks once again impacted the world.

Summary

Greek culture lives in Western culture. Greek democracy, philosophy and science, drama, their ways of investigating, analyzing, and reporting events, and their ways of managing and executing war strategies are only some of the things that continue to impact Western culture.

Greek thinking, combined with some of the fundamental ideas of Judaism, provide a substantial segment of the foundation of Western civilization. A third element that underlies Western culture is Christianity. We will look more closely at its contribution in the next chapter.

Chapter 4

The Development and Expansion
Of Christianity

The World into Which Christianity Was Born

Christianity was born into the world of Hellenism. Hellenistic culture was a *Greek-like* culture that dominated the Middle East after the death of Alexander the Great in 323 BC. Alexander's quest to conquer included spreading Greek culture to the regions he vanquished. The Greek language served as the primary vehicle for disseminating the Greek culture, which included Greek thinking regarding religion, politics and government, society, philosophy, literature and rhetoric, art, mathematics and science. Greek culture was the most advanced, refined culture of the ancient world. Its spread during Alexander's brief reign changed the ancient world by providing people with new ways of thinking and behaving, and, for some, even altering their underlying worldview assumptions.

After Alexander's death, four of his generals divided up his empire among themselves, establishing geopolitical entities that maintained control until those territories were eventually conquered by the Romans. Antiochus III, who ruled Syria (which included Greece and the surrounding territory) was finally defeated by the Romans in 189 BC.

As noted earlier, the Romans borrowed many cultural practices from the Greeks, modifying some of them as they did. It is impossible to speak of either a purely Greek or Roman culture during this time. Thus the cultural context of that day is often referred to as *Greco-Roman*. In 14 AD the Roman Empire consisted of many different ethnic groups who spoke dozens of different languages. While there were approximately 5 million citizens of Rome in 14 AD, there were about 50 million people who inhabited Roman controlled territories. The Roman Empire was really a conglomeration of cultures, so a general cultural designation beyond *Hellenistic* is not possible.

The First Century Jewish Context

The Jewish people experienced many governmental changes from the time they returned from captivity (536 BC) to the time the first Christian community was established in 30 AD. They had lived under Persian rule until Alexander came with his conquering armies (332-323 BC). After Alexander's death when his generals divided up his empire among themselves, the Jews experienced the rule of the Ptolemies and the Seleucides, which culminated in the reign of Antiochus IV. When Antiochus tried to destroy the Jewish religion, he ran into more resistance than he imagined possible. The Maccabean revolt (167 BC) amounted to a protracted, small scale war with the Seleucides until 142 BC, when a force led by a Jew named Simon finally defeated them. The Jews enjoyed a measure of freedom until infighting and civil war brought the Romans in 63 BC (Ferguson 1967:37-67; Martin 1975:53-83). The world in which Jesus lived and died, and in which Christianity was established (during the first third of the first century AD) was a world of Jewish law and tradition, including temple, synagogue, holy days, celebrations, fasting, sociopolitical unrest, religious sects, and dozens of day-to-day concerns that were part of daily life in the first century Jewish context. In this section we will examine a few of them briefly. (Anne Punton provides an excellent overview of daily life in first century Palestine in *The World Jesus Knew*, 2002.)

In the broadest sense, Jewish society was agrarian. The Jewish economy was rooted in farming and livestock. That does not mean, however, that all Jews were farmers. While many worked the land, growing wheat, barley or other grains, grapes, olives or figs, some were craftsmen, such as carpenters. Others were fishermen. Some were merchants. They had what amounted to a craftsmen-based middle class. Generally speaking, though, they were hardworking people of the land.

They were a family oriented people who considered children a blessing from God and who enjoyed having large families. Firstborn sons were dedicated to God, symbolizing that the child was a blessing from God and that ultimately all things belonged to God. Jewish parents were loving parents who took God's instructions to educate their children in his ways very seriously (Deut. 6:1-9).

Education began early in a child's life. Children would observe and learn from the weekly traditions observed by their family. For instance, the prayers and blessings related to the Sabbath meal, spoken by their father each Friday evening, educated children about God. They would learn the importance of obedience to God by noticing that (and asking why) their father touched the *mezuzah* each time he went in or out of his house. The *mezuzah* was a small piece of parchment with scriptures written on it (Deut. 6:4-9, 11:13-21). It was placed in a container and attached to the doorpost as a reminder of the importance of obedience to God and of teaching one's children to obey. Phylacteries served a similar purpose. Phylacteries were small boxes attached on a headband or armband. Small portions of Scripture would be written down and placed in the small box which was then worn on the arm or the forehead as a reminder of God's law. A child's curiosity as to what the little boxes were and why people wore them would provide parents with teaching opportunities.

The Jews took their obligation to teach their children so seriously that it was against the law to live in a community without a school. Communities with twenty-five students were required to appoint a schoolmaster. If there were fifty students an assistant schoolmaster was also required. Children had to learn three languages: Hebrew, the language of Scripture, Aramaic, the common language in Palestine, and Greek, the common language of the empire. At age ten, boys began to study the Torah—the Jewish law contained in the first five books of the Hebrew Scriptures.

Jewish homes were built close together, usually out of mud bricks. The typical Israelite house may have been a two-story house with four rooms built around a central courtyard. The living and sleeping areas were upstairs. The flat roof was accessible by a stairway outside the house and was used to dry fruits, and often for sleeping on hot summer nights (Selman 1998:Vol. 2, 668-672).

Jewish society did not distinguish between the secular and the sacred. Their view of life was holistic. Everything was in some way connected to everything else. Religious ceremony and tradition permeated their lives. Their interactions with others (especially non-Jewish people) were studiously monitored so as to avoid defilement. A simple trip to the market required ceremonial washings afterward to insure ongoing ceremonial cleanness. There were dietary regulations. Certain foods had to be avoided. Foods had to be prepared in specified ways. Utensils and containers had to be washed and carefully maintained. On one level, symbols of religious purity were understood for what they were—symbols. But at the same time, on another level, those symbols, as far as the Jews understood from the Hebrew Scriptures, were so closely associated with the spiritual realities themselves that to fail in regard to the symbol was to fail in regard to the reality. Traditions, therefore, related to the symbolism of purity were dominant factors in their lives.

There were three religious feasts each year that were major features of Jewish life: Passover (in April), Pentecost (in June) and the Feast of Tabernacles (in September). Unless there were serious mitigating circumstances, all Jewish males over twenty years old were required to attend these feasts in Jerusalem.

Temple worship was the focal point of Jewish spiritual life. The temple was God's symbolic house, symbolizing his presence among his people. Originally, the Ark of the Covenant had been housed in the temple. No one knows when or under what circumstances it was taken away. Most likely it was carried off by conquerors. By the first century it had been gone from the Jerusalem temple for a long time. As unfortunate as that may have been, the temple itself (rebuilt several times since the original structure had been completed by Solomon) remained the focal point of Jewish worship. Daily sacrifices and prayers were conducted by the priests and worshippers were continually present (McKelvey 1998:Vol. 3, 1522-1532).

The synagogue was another major feature of daily life in first century Palestine. The synagogue had not been ordained by God. But the Israelites (most likely while in captivity, their temple having been destroyed) decided they needed a place of regular worship (Meyers 1992:Vol. 6, 251-260). The synagogue was designed to meet that need. A cross between a church and a religious community center, the synagogue was a place of worship, fellowship, education, and "government of the civil life of the community" (Feinberg 1998:Vol. 3, 1499-1503).

Every Jewish community of any size had a synagogue. The weekly assembly consisted of Scripture readings, an expository lesson based on that week's scheduled reading, prayers, and songs. A synagogue manager was responsible for organizing all synagogue activities.

The Jewish social context was very religious. But it was far from a perfect society. The religious leaders were often guilty of hypocrisy. They were often unjust. There was poverty and suffering. Marginalized people—women, the sick, poor, children, the uneducated, and those who were considered "sinful" people—had few rights and even fewer opportunities to change their unequal, unhappy circumstances.

Such was the Jewish cultural context into which Jesus came and in which Christianity was established.

The First Century Hellenistic Context

While Christianity was established within and as a part of the Jewish socioreligious context, it was not long (approximately ten years) before the Christian message (a message of freedom from a life of sin and reconciliation with God through faith in Jesus) began to spread among non-Jewish people. As the "good news" about reconciliation with God spread into the Hellenistic world, what cultural phenomena were encountered?

As noted earlier, the Hellenistic period dates roughly from the third century BC to the first century AD. The sociocultural context of the first century Hellenistic world was similar to and at the same time very different from the first century Jewish culture of Palestine. It was similar in that the Hellenistic world was also agrarian. They lived off the land, farming and herding. To be sure, there were craftsmen and merchants who did not farm, but farming and food production was the backbone of Hellenistic society.

People married and had families. Parents loved their children. They educated and trained them to be socially responsible and productive. They were religious people. From this perspective of broad cultural strokes it is possible to discuss the similarities between Palestinian and Hellenistic society. Indeed, such generalized comparisons can be made between almost any groups of people. However, when one looks closely, the differences between Jewish and Hellenistic social contexts are significant.

The term *Hellenistic culture* should not be understood to imply that all cultures influenced by Hellenism were alike. Numerous and varied cultures existed within the Hellenistic world. Individual cultures were impacted by Hellenism and in the process were changed to varying degrees. But they retained their own unique feel and pulse. The Hellenistic world was not monolithic—that is, it was not a single culture (Starr 1991:431). It was pluralistic—made up of many cultures and cultural perspectives.

The Hellenistic world was also polytheistic. The ancient Greek pantheon had included twelve important gods and goddesses. Many of these retained their significance in Hellenistic culture, though eventually they were given Latin names. For example, the Latin god Jupiter may simply have been a borrowing and renaming of the Greek god Zeus.

These gods were very "human" in nature and character, displaying selfish, brutal tendencies, including betrayal, murder, sexual immorality, and the like. Religion based on or directed to such depraved deities tended to reflect those qualities rather than the holiness of the one true God who had made himself known to Abraham and his descendents. People who worshipped depraved gods had no reason to improve their behavior. They were already as good as the gods they worshipped. And if they were to aspire to loftier standards they had no example of what those might be or how to achieve them.

Another "religious" phenomenon of the Hellenistic world into which Christianity was born was cult worship. Cult worship involved the elevation of a ruler to the status of a god. This may have been done simply as an act of flattery, or to provide an insurance policy against the ruler's displeasure, or in an attempt to get things done (Freeman 1996:280). Whatever the reason, cult worship was another form of idolatry.

A form of idolatry that existed at least in some places (such as Corinth) involved sexual intercourse with temple prostitutes (Ferguson 1993:261). Worshipers would offer a traditional sacrifice and then select a temple prostitute (a young woman who had volunteered to serve the deity) who specialized in a specific sexual activity.

Urbanism was an important feature of Hellenistic culture (280-282). The ethnocentric imperialism of Alexander the Great involved not only conquering other peoples to expand Greek holdings, but also to export what he considered a superior culture across the earth. The focus of Greek culture—art, philosophy, government, and generally speaking, the good life—was especially suited to life in the city. The city-state had evolved in Greece and as Alexander raced from campaign to campaign, cities sprang up in his wake. Throughout the Hellenistic period, cities, and all that goes with urban life, continued to emerge.

While cities in one region may have differed from cities in another region (they were allowed to retain their own cultural distinctiveness) the pressure to be assimilated into Greek culture was immense. It was simply expected that one would learn to speak like, think like, and act like a Greek—which, as noted previously, included attending the theater, demonstrating allegiance to the Greek cults, and stripping naked to exercise at the gymnasium (Freeman 1996:282).

Another development of Hellenism, though one not easily explained, is the emergence of a new class of wealthy people. Freeman notes that it was not that the Mediterranean world itself became a place of greater wealth, but that what wealth there was seemed to have been redistributed into the hands of a new group of people—a wealthy business class (282-283).

Slavery was a major consideration of Hellenistic culture. It is estimated that there were two to three million slaves in Italy (40 percent of the population) at the end of the first century BC (Freeman 1996:455-456). "Slaves and their children were the property of their owners, to be treated like any other commodity," (Adkins and Adkins 1994:341-342). Some, especially household slaves who may have been tutors for children or estate managers, were treated quite well. Others were treated brutally, kept in chains, beaten, or sexually abused. Slavery was one of the darkest aspects of the otherwise enlightened Hellenistic perspective.

The sanctity of marriage was not held in high esteem in the Hellenistic culture. There was no stigma attached to divorce. Morality in general was not an important consideration. "It was taken for granted that men would make use of a mistress, a slave, or a prostitute" (340). "Abortion was practiced for unwanted pregnancies" and "newborn children could be killed, sold or exposed" (340).

As noted earlier, upon close inspection the differences between Jewish culture and Hellenistic culture were significant. Though Christianity was born into a Jewish cultural context, it spread into the larger Hellenistic world, encountering a culture that was rooted in very different assumptions. The challenges faced by Christianity were enormous.

The Impact of Christianity on the Roman Empire

As noted earlier, the Roman world was very cosmopolitan. Cities sprang up across the Greco-Roman landscape allowing for an expansive healthy commerce. The

Pax Romana (the peace and subsequent safety made possible by Roman military domination) made the world a safe place. Travel over well-maintained roads that connected major cities made travel as easy as it could be in that day. Around 150 AD, a Roman gentleman named Aelius Aristides commented on the ease and safety of travel under Roman rule:

> A man simply travels from one country to another as though it were his native land. We are no longer frightened by the Cilician pass or by the narrow sand tracks that lead from Arabia into Egypt. We are not dismayed by the height of the mountains, or by the vast breadth of rivers or by the inhospitable tribes of barbarians. To be a Roman citizen, nay even one of [the emperor's] subjects, is a sufficient guarantee of personal safety, (Spickard and Cragg 1994:43).

The Romans knew how to manage and control land and people. The social order they brought made the world safe. But their focus on *the good of Rome above all else* was a double-edged sword. Anything that appeared to be a threat to Roman rule met an immediate and often brutal response. Unfortunately, for dozens of decades Christianity was perceived as a threat to Roman security. How? Why? The following sections will answer those questions and demonstrate how Christianity overcame significant obstacles to become the dominant force in Western culture at that time.

A Difficult Beginning

According to the book of Acts (2:47, 4:4, 5:12-16), the first believers were held in high esteem by their fellow Jews—at least among the general population. But in a short period of time the esteem turned to animosity and Jews who believed Jesus was God's messiah were persecuted by Jews who did not. Robert Williams notes that the persecution of Christians can be broken into three phases: 1) Jewish

71

persecution of Christians, from Jesus' death to the great fire in Rome—AD 64, 2) Roman persecution instigated by society, AD 64-250, and 3) Roman persecution initiated by the government, AD 250-313 (1999:895-899). While the Jewish population in general (and at first) may have held Jesus' followers in high esteem, the religious leaders appear to have been antagonistic toward the movement from the beginning. This is most likely what Williams has in mind in suggesting that Jewish persecution began at Jesus' death.

Jewish persecution was so intense that believers had to flee, leaving the region around Jerusalem for areas where it was safe to practice their faith (Ac. 8:1-4). At first, as Jewish believers spread out into other areas of the Hellenistic world they avoided interaction with non-Jewish people. Minimizing contact with non-Jewish people in an effort to avoid ceremonial uncleanness had been a hallmark of their society for ages. Eventually, however, through a special prompting by God (Acts 10:1-23), the Jewish believers began telling the story of Jesus and reconciliation with God to non-Jewish people. As the believers began to impact the city of Antioch, Syria, the people of the region who had not responded favorably to the message about Jesus began to refer to the believers as *Christians* (Acts 11:26) because they believed Jesus was the Christ. The term Christ is the Greek world for Hebrew term *messiah,* which means the one sent by God. Referring to those who believed in Jesus as *Christians* was not a complimentary designation, but it was accurate. Eventually even believers began to refer to themselves as Christians (1 Peter 4:14-16) because they were, in fact, followers of Christ.

Since the first believers were Jewish, the Romans assumed that Christianity was one of several Jewish sects. When the unbelieving Jews realized what was happening, they made it very clear that, as far as they were concerned, Christians were not part of the Jewish community. It was around 65 AD that the Romans realized that Christianity, though it had begun as an outgrowth of Judaism, was not a sect of Judaism (Spickard and Cragg 1994:40). It was a new and powerful faith movement that they did not understand.

As Williams had suggested, the persecution of Christians by Romans (between 64-250) was not a concerted effort instigated by the government. It was more a matter of private citizens complaining about individuals who were known to be Christians. There were two basic reasons for Roman animosity toward Christians: 1) misunderstanding about beliefs and practices, and 2) resentment toward the Christians' unwillingness to honor the many gods recognized throughout the Empire.

Christian terminology concerning the *Eucharist*, which literally means *thanksgiving* and refers to the weekly communion, was misunderstood. The bread and wine of Christian communion represents Jesus' body and blood. However, it is often spoken of in literal sounding language *as* the body and blood of Jesus. This led outsiders to conclude that the Christians were guilty of barbaric acts of cannibalism—eating human flesh and drinking human blood. In a similar way, terminology related to the *love feast* was misunderstood by unbelievers. The love feast referred to a fellowship meal believers enjoyed as a part of their weekly worship assembly. Because believers referred to fellow Christians as brothers and sisters, those who were not part of the Christian community misunderstood, thinking that the love feast was some sort of incestuous orgy. Such misunderstandings regarding Christian beliefs and practices led to a prejudice against believers.

This prejudice was then intensified by the Christians' unwillingness to honor the gods of the empire. Not honoring the gods with sacrifices and offerings—at least giving them occasional lip service—would offend them, resulting in calamities of all sorts. Whenever problems arose within the empire, Christians were blamed. The citizenry concluded that the gods were angry because the Christians refused to honor them. This resulted in a great deal of animosity toward the Christians. Therefore, if someone was known to be a Christian they would be turned in to the authorities, who would arrest them. They were arrested not for their religious beliefs *per se*, but because their actions were interpreted as traitorous. Actions that did not put the empire ahead of all other allegiances were subject to severe treatment. To cause problems for Rome was to be a traitor to Rome. Behavior which set the gods against the empire was clearly unacceptable behavior. The New Testament refers to persecution in the form of having personal property confiscated, imprisonment, and even death.

The disdain many Romans felt toward Christians is communicated effectively in a quote from Celsus (178 AD):

> Intellectually, their doctrine was nothing more than a new perversion and corruption of ancient tradition. Socially, this disagreeably non-conformist organization was characterized by such evil and strange practices as incest and cannibalism. Its hatred of all humanity was legendary. Politically, Christians were atheists who despised the ancient gods, undermining and threatening the structure and stability of society and government (Spickard and Cragg 1994:44-45).

Times of persecution may have come in waves, increasing and then decreasing in intensity. An ancient letter between Pliny, a local official, and the Emperor Trajan (who ruled from 98-117) indicates that the trials of Christians, at least at that time, were not common place. Pliny wrote to Trajan asking his advice as to how to proceed because he had never witnessed a trial against a Christian. Trajan's advice was to not actively seek out Christians, and to give them a chance to deny being a Christian before carrying out punishment if they were exposed as such by Roman citizens (40-41). This kind of persecution was carried out against Christians for over 180 years.

In the third phase of Christian persecution (AD 250-313), as Williams has outlined it, the government began to actively pursue believers. For many, the empire was becoming too Christian. Henry Chadwick notes that "by 250 the church was freely penetrating the upper levels of Roman society" (1992:42). This made the unbelievers uncomfortable. Rome was beginning to experience difficulties in the outlying regions. Leaders who believed the problems to be the retaliation of angry gods sought to restore the traditional Roman gods to their former preeminent positions. Their goal was to get rid of the Christians and strengthen the ancient religions (paganism) that had been weakened by the spread of Christianity.

The campaign to eradicate Christianity intensified over time and by the spring of 304 Galerius demanded that all people sacrifice to the gods (and the emperor) or be put to death (Williams 1999:898). With the coming of Constantine, however, everything changed. In 312 or 313 he issued an edict of toleration lifting the ban against Christianity (Todd 1990:140-144; Hinson 1996:198-201). Though Christians represented a minority in the empire's population at that time, Constantine's "acceptance" of Christianity allowed freedom of belief (and expression of that belief) which led to a popular acceptance of Christianity in general. By the end of the fourth century, the majority of the empire's population claimed to be Christian. It must be noted, however, that claiming to be a Christian does not mean that one actually is a Christian.

Scholars have long debated whether Christianity's rapid spread after Constantine's edict represented a true, complete, sincere conversion to the Christian faith or merely a popular *pagan-like* acceptance of a new religion. Ultimately, only God can answer that question. Most likely some conversions were genuine and some were not. However, whether or not the Christian faith was completely embraced and internalized by all who claimed allegiance to

Christ, there were surface-level behaviors that were put in place that reflected the presence of the Christian faith. Pagan temples were eventually closed and idols were destroyed. Church buildings were built and in time the pagan Roman Empire had become the Christian Roman Empire. How had this happened? What factors gave Christianity is strength and appeal?

Slow but Steady Progress

There had always been godly Hellenists in the Greco-Roman world. During Jesus' ministry in Palestine there were non-Jewish people who had been attracted to the high moral standards, the monotheistic theology, and the hope inherent in Judaism. Some of them had been fully converted to Judaism, embracing Jewish culture completely. Others, though not fully converted, had embraced much of the theology and life of Judaism. These people were known as *God-fearers*. When Christian mission teams, such as Paul and Barnabas, traveled throughout the empire telling the story of Jesus in the early second half of the first century, there were nearly always Gentile converts and God-fearers associated with Jewish synagogues. Many of these very spiritual people eagerly believed and embraced the message about Jesus and reconciliation with God.

But even people who had not previously been interested in a monotheistic faith found themselves drawn to the Christian faith. Why? There are two basic reasons. One was the message, the other was the life.

The Christian Message

Hinson notes that "a profound fatalism gripped the minds of most persons in the ancient world" (1996:27). There were more slaves in the Roman world than there were Roman citizens. Beyond the glories of the empire there was little to hold on to. There was no hope in life. The gods were to be feared. Death was to be feared. Life was simply to be lived. And when life is lived in fear and day after day is filled with the dull hopelessness of nothing better to look forward to, a message of hope, faith, love, security, and a better life is bound to attract some attention.

The gospel was an amazing story. In the person of Jesus, God had become a human being. Having planned his own death as a sacrifice of atonement, he offered himself so he could forgive and save his sinful human children. He died for all people—young, old, men, women, sick, weak, strong, free, slave, poor—it didn't matter. All were welcome. All were equal. All were loved. All were accepted. All could have hope for life after death—a better life than they could even imagine. Clement, a Christian who lived in Alexandria, Egypt, noted that: "All our life is a celebration for us. . . We sing while we work, we sing hymns while we sail, we pray while we carry out all life's other occupations" (Collins and Price 1999:49). The "good news" about Jesus was good because it offered hope; it made life better. The Christian message was very appealing.

The Christian Life

But there was more to the Christian message than hope for the future. Embracing the Christian faith meant incorporation and participation in a community of faith. It meant being accepted and loved, cared for and valued as a person who had been created in the image of the eternal God. It meant having standards by which to live—God's standards. Christians were to be morally upright. Sexual immorality was simply not acceptable. Christians were to be honest and hardworking. Christian wives were to be submissive to their husbands. Christian husbands were to love their wives. Husbands and wives were to honor their marriage obligations and remain faithful to each other.

Christian children were to honor and obey their parents. Christian slaves were to be obedient and hardworking. Christian masters were to be kind to their slaves. Christians were to obey civil law, pay taxes and honor government officials. They were to be kind, generous, productive, helpful, happy, caring people. And most were.

Christian worship, as part of the Christian lifestyle, was another appealing factor. Christians assembled each week to enjoy each other's company, to honor God and to be taught and encouraged. Their assemblies were simple. In the early days before Constantine's edict, most Christian assemblies were in believer's homes. They would sing, pray, listen as Scripture was read and as a lesson was presented. They would commune together, eating bread and drinking wine, which symbolized Jesus' body and blood which he had sacrificed for them. Their times together were precious. Masters and slaves ate and worshipped together as equals, as brothers and sisters, children of their heavenly Father. If any of them had needs, the rest would find ways to help them. What little they had they shared with each other. In one of his letters, Tertullian, a believer who lived 155-222, referred to a common pagan observation regarding the Christian community: "See how those Christians love one another." The Emperor Julian, who reigned briefly from 361-363 and who hated Christians, admitted that Christianity had been advanced 1) through the loving service of Christians to strangers, and 2) through the care they exhibited in burying their dead (Collins and Price 1999:49).

Impacting an Empire

The combination of the Christian message and the Christian life is what appealed to the people of the Greco-Roman world. Christianity began with 120 people on a Sunday morning in Jerusalem in 30 AD. By the end of the fourth century it held the Roman Empire in the palm of its hand. What an accomplishment! But what, exactly, had been accomplished? What had happened? And who was responsible for what had happened?

What happened was that people were converted. They were changed. They began to think differently, which led to different behaviors. Their values changed. Their outlook on life changed. When a few people experience a dramatic, life-altering conversion it does not normally impact society as a whole. But when thousands, and then tens of thousands, and then millions of people experience fundamental changes at the deepest levels of being, the society of which they are a part will also be altered. That is what happened to the Greco-Roman world between 30 and 400 AD. So many people were converted to Christianity that the culture as a whole was changed. It went from being fundamentally pagan to fundamentally Christian. This does not mean that everyone in the society understood Christianity, experienced a genuine conversion and lived the kind of life God wanted them to live. That was clearly not the case. However, enough people did experience a genuine conversion, understood enough of Christianity, and lived close enough to what God wanted so that the Roman world was impacted in a positive way. The kinds of changes that occurred in the Roman world can be illustrated with a few examples.

Christianity's Impact on Paganism

Christianity began to impact Greco-Roman culture almost immediately. The events that occurred in the ancient city of Ephesus as a result of the preaching of the Christian message (as recorded by Luke in Acts 19) are illustrative of the initial impact of Christianity. As a result of the missionary efforts of the apostle Paul and his mission team, many people in the region of Ephesus were converted, abandoning their pagan religions. They burned their books of magic spells and incantations that were part of their religious practices. Sales of household idols dropped off dramatically. The local guild of silversmiths, who made their living chiefly from making small household idols, experienced such a drop in income that they became outraged and incited a riot, claiming that Paul's preaching was diminishing the glory and reputation of their local goddess Artemis (also known as Diana). The riot was so disruptive that local city officials feared that Roman troops would be dispatched to quell the disturbance. The officials were finally able to quiet and disburse the angry crowd, narrowly avoiding an Imperial response.

This happened in the early years of Christianity (in the late 50s) when relatively few people (compared to the entire population) had been converted to Christianity. Imagine the impact two hundred years later when the percentage of the population being converted increased substantially.

Christianity's impact on paganism was significant because a people's religious beliefs represent a fundamental feature of their worldview, of their basic underlying assumptions of reality and life in this world. When a person's deep-level worldview assumptions about religion are changed—assumptions about the supernatural, about birth, life, and death—a number of other fundamental changes occur as well. Fundamental changes in religious beliefs lead to fundamental changes in how one lives life.

Christianity's Impact on Morality

The ancient city of Corinth and the church there provide an example of how changes in religious beliefs result in changes in lifestyle. When the apostle Paul, who established the church in that city, wrote to them, he reminded them of the changes they had experienced as a result of their Christian faith:

> *Don't you know that those who do wrong will have no share in the Kingdom of God? Don't fool yourselves. Those who indulge in sexual sin, who are idol worshipers, adulterers, male prostitutes, homosexuals, thieves, greedy people, drunkards, abusers, and swindlers--none of these will have a share in the Kingdom of God. There was a time when some of you were just like that, but now your sins have been washed away, and you have been set apart for God. You have been made right with God because of what the Lord Jesus Christ and the Spirit of our God have done for you* (1 Corinthians 6:9-11).

Corinth had a reputation of being a wicked city. Sexual immorality was rampant. Worship to the goddess Aphrodite involved having sex with a temple prostitute. The city's reputation was so bad that even in ancient times it gave rise to the term to *Corinthianize*, that is, to practice fornication (Oster 1993:134-135). The Christians in Corinth had been idolatrous, immoral people. But something had happened to them. Something had occurred in their lives that resulted in a fundamental change in they way they lived their lives. They had become Christians. A portion of their worldview had been altered. They had acquired a new perspective on life. They had developed a new set of values and moral standards by which they lived. The Christians in Corinth were certainly not perfect people. Far from it. But they were different people. They had been changed in good and beneficial ways, in ways that benefited their families and society, making the city of Corinth a better place to live.

Part of the Christian conversion included a new way of thinking and acting toward others. Not only did people stop lying, cheating, stealing, and living immoral lives, they became kind, generous, loving people. As noted earlier, even among the pagans who hated them, Christians were known as loving people. They would not share their beds, but they would share their bread. They would not steal from others, but they would gladly share what little they had with those who had even less.

Christianity impacted the pagan religions of the Roman world. It impacted the morality of the empire, and, eventually, as the numbers of believers in the general population increased, Christianity also impacted the government.

Christianity's Impact on the Government

The Christians of the Roman Empire did not seek political reform. They had no political agenda. In fact, believers went to great lengths not to cause political problems. Paul had taught Christian wives to be submissive to their husbands, Christian children to respect, honor, and obey their parents, and Christian slaves to be obedient, hardworking, and productive for their masters (Ephesians 5:21-6:9). He had also taught respect for government officials and obedience to civil law:

> *Obey the government, for God is the one who put it there. All governments have been placed in power by God. So those who refuse to obey the laws of the land are refusing to obey God, and punishment will follow. For the authorities do not frighten people who are doing right, but they frighten those who do wrong. So do what they say, and you will get along well. The authorities are sent by God to help you. But if you are doing something wrong, of course you should be afraid, for you will be punished. The authorities are established by God for that very purpose, to punish those who do wrong. So you must obey the government for two reasons: to keep from being punished and to keep a clear conscience. Pay your taxes, too, for these same reasons. For government workers need to be paid so they can keep on doing the work God intended them to do. Give to everyone what you owe them: Pay your taxes and import duties, and give respect and honor to all to whom it is due* (Romans 13:1-7).

Those early believers were not subversives. They were not revolutionaries. They did not seek to overthrow the government. They sent no delegations to the emperors in an

82

attempt to gain a more favorable sociopolitical environment. They wanted nothing more than to live out their faith in peace and service to others. However, when the percentage of the population who espouse a given belief increases, especially among the wealthy, privileged of society, wise officials will pay attention to the needs and opinions of those people.

Christianity and Ancient Western Culture

When Constantine believed he had received a vision from God instructing him to carry out his military campaign in the name of Christ, and when he and Licinius, ruler of the eastern empire, issued the edict of toleration (Irvin and Sunquist 2001:162), Christianity became socially acceptable. Though the majority of the empire's population remained pagan until after the middle of the fourth century (Chadwick 1993:152), since the Emperor himself seemed open to Christianity (though Constantine did not personally embrace Christianity until just before his death) the floodgates of conversion opened and many who had not previously responded to the Gospel openly embraced Christianity.

As a result of Christianity's widespread acceptance, a number of significant cultural shifts gradually manifested themselves:

1) church leaders became exempt from imperial taxes,
2) the Christian symbol of the cross was put on the shields of the Roman soldiers,
3) Sunday, the Christian day of worship, was designated a weekly holiday (holy day) so Christians could worship without having to schedule their activities around work,
4) the name of Christ began to appear on Roman coinage along with the Emperor's name,
5) church buildings were funded and built,
6) the calendar began to change—pagan holidays being deleted and Christian celebrations being included, and
7) the church began to be linked to the State in an official way
(Irvin and Sunquist 2110:163-164).

Whether all these changes were good or not, such as the linkage of church and state, is not the focus of this study. The point under consideration is the dramatic impact Christianity had on the Roman Empire—an impact that became long-range and far-reaching. There can be little doubt that the Roman Empire was deeply affected by the presence of Christianity. And to say that the Roman Empire was deeply affected by the presence of Christianity is to say that Western society and culture (civilization) was deeply affected by the presence of Christianity.

We have noted already the impact of Judaism on Western culture. We discussed *monotheism*, *moral absolutes*, the importance of *social justice*, and a social orientation that is *guilt-justice* rather than shame-honor. These were features of ancient Judaism and their prominence in Western culture can be traced to Ancient Israel. However, their presence in Western culture is a reality because they are features of Judaism that were absorbed (along with others) into Christianity and passed on to the West because of Christianity's impact on the Roman Empire. In other words, the Jewish beliefs that have impacted the West so thoroughly have done so not because they were originally Jewish, but because they became Christian beliefs.

In what other ways did Christianity, in its Imperial Roman context, impact Western culture? With its focus on love for all, including enemies, and non-retaliation, the society gradually became less brutal and aggressive. Some historians, both ancient and modern, saw this softening of the Roman harshness as a contributing factor in the ultimate collapse of empire. While that may be an over statement, there is no doubt that Christianity's focus on love and gentleness did impact the society.

Christianity also impacted Roman society in relation to morals and ethics. Christianity teaches believers to be morally and ethically upright, to grow and change, to be concerned about personal holiness. Honesty and integrity are important in Christian societies. So when millions of people who were part of the Roman Empire became Christians and were confronted with the need to change, naturally the social make-up of the empire was impacted.

If Christianity was (is) a religion of love for all people, then service to others is part of the Christian ethos. As noted earlier, even opponents of Christianity had to admit that they were kind, generous people who shared what they had with those less fortunate.

Christians were hardworking, peaceful, obedient people who wanted only to serve their Lord in peace. It was their humble but firm resolve to be obedient to God and helpful to others that changed individual lives and eventually an empire.

Summary

Christianity sprang up from Jewish roots during the early days of the Roman Empire. Christianity and the Empire grew up together in an uneasy relationship. At first, for a brief time, Christianity was viewed positively by Jewish society. But then things turned sour and Jews who did not believe Jesus was God's messiah began to persecute those who did believe. Initially, Rome was indifferent toward Christianity, but when it became apparent that Christians would not worship the many gods of the Empire, the Roman people and then the government began to persecute Christians. The Jews would not worship the gods of the empire either. But it was the Christians who were persecuted for this.

Christians, however, were firm in their resolve and refused to be turned from their faith. Eventually, their kindness in the face of brutality won over the citizenry and when the Emperor Constantine issued his edict of toleration, signaling his acceptance of Christianity, many people embraced the faith. Some of those conversions were genuine. Some were half-hearted, and uninformed. Many people who claimed to be Christians were not. But enough people genuinely embraced the faith and changed their lives so that the makeup of Roman society was also changed. A pagan society became a Christian society. It was a weak and wavering Christian society with many confused and inconsistent ideas and behaviors, but a society that had begun moving in the right direction.

Eventually, as Rome's internal structures began to falter and opponents from without forced their will on a weakening Roman military, Christianity maintained its vibrant influence. As Rome stumbled, Christianity stood resolute. In its struggle with Rome, Christianity had emerged as victor. And while Rome would crumble in the dust, Christianity would develop the European West into a world power. Christianity had impacted the Roman Empire. Now it was poised to shape the Western world. The next chapter will demonstrate how Christianity continued to be a factor in the shaping of the West, including blending Christian theology and Greek philosophy in a way that made the Renaissance and the Enlightenment possible, thus laying the foundation for the Western culture we know today.

Chapter 5

The Collapse of the Empire,   ·
The Rise of the Church

The Coming of the Barbarians

The Romans considered their culture the standard by which all other cultures should be measured. As far as they were concerned, their society epitomized the height of civilization. Other societies were looked down on as less civilized. Many were considered as simply barbaric. Whether they learned to think this way from the Greeks or whether this kind of arrogance is typical of powerful people is open to discussion. But the Romans felt superior to those who were different from them.

Among the peoples the Romans considered barbaric were the Germanic tribes that had been a threat on the empire's eastern frontier for centuries. The Germanic tribes that troubled the Romans were descendants of ancient Nordic peoples that migrated south in the 5th century BC, though Norman Cantor suggests that the migrations may have been occurring as early as 1000 BC (1994:90). The Cimbri and the Teutons, originally from Jutland (which is now known as Denmark) migrated southward together.

Eventually the two peoples separated with the Teutons settling the area known as Gaul. In 102 BC they were annihilated in battle by the Romans. Even though they were defeated by the large, well-train Roman army, they were a fierce people, so much so that when the Teuton women saw that the battle was lost, they killed their children and then themselves rather than be taken by the enemy.

The later Germanic tribes that troubled the Roman Empire (the Goths, Visigoths, the Ostrogoths, and Vandals) were descendants of the Nordic Teutons and Cimbri, as were the Vikings. Little is known of the specific religions of the Goths before their clash with the Roman Empire. However, it is safe to assume that since they were descendants of the Teutons and Cimbri, their religious beliefs were similar to the beliefs and practices of other peoples who were also descendants of the Teutons and the Cimbri—namely the Vikings.

Ancient Nordic Religion

Nordic (or Scandinavian) traditional religion has much in common with other forms of ancient paganism. There was a pantheon of gods and goddesses, including: Odin, the king of the gods, Thor, the god of thunder, Loki, who represented evil, Hel, goddess of the dead, and the Valkyries, warrior maidens who attended Odin. They were not necessarily all-powerful, all-knowing, or even always good in their behavior. Like the Greek and Romans gods, Nordic deities had "*human-like*," characteristics, which was common of many pagan deities since they were products of human imagination. Greater or lesser deities would be worshipped through prescribed rituals involving priests and sacrifices. Sometimes the sacrifices were human.

Even if the Goths used different names for the specific gods they worshipped, it seems likely that their traditional religion would have developed along lines similar to their ethnic cousins the Vikings. Preben Meulengracht Sørensen provides an excellent overview of ancient Nordic religion (1997:205-218).

Generally speaking, then, the Goths were like other ancient pagan people, worshipping a number of different gods depending on their needs at a given time. Their worship would have involved sacrifices designed to earn a god's favor. In some circumstances the sacrifice may have been a human being. Moral standards were not linked to their religious practices. Paganism (of any kind) has little to do with becoming a better person. It has to do with the manipulation of power. Because pagan religions had little relation to morality, pagan society may or may not have enjoyed a highly developed moral and ethical structure. Those societies that enjoyed a more fully developed moral and ethical structure did so not because of religious convictions, but because they had discovered that a morally disciplined society simply worked better than a morally lax society. Evidently the Germanic tribes that troubled the Roman Empire had not yet discovered the benefits of a morally and ethically disciplined society. They were pagan and they were brutish.

Cantor notes, however, that the Ostrogoths, the people closest to the Danube, the eastern border of the empire, had more interaction with the Romans and had become less brutish in their manner. The tribes, however, that remained further removed from contact with the Romans continued to be less refined in their manner (1994:90).

Missionaries among the Barbarians

The cycle of barbarian invasion and Roman response was a continuous reality for centuries. In the mid-third century, Cappadocia was invaded by Gothic warriors who captured and dragged off many Christians as their prisoners. Among those captured were the parents (or grandparents) of

Ulfilas—a man who later became the "apostle" to the Goths. According to Chadwick (1993:151), it was Ulfilas' grandparents who were captured. Their son or daughter then married a Visigoth and had a child they named Ulfilas (or Ulfila). In 341, Ulfilas entered the empire as a member of the Gothic embassy. He had been raised as a Christian, although he accepted the Arian view of Christ's nature and person. At that time the Arian controversy (a false doctrine which argued that Jesus was not fully God but only a created being) had not yet been resolved and Eusebius of Nicomedia, along with a number of other bishops, consecrated Ulfilas, making him a bishop, and sent him to work among the Goths (Chadwick 1993:248-249). As a result of his work, many of the Goths became Christians, although it was the Arian form of Christianity—which was later to be branded a heresy.

In time, the church sent additional missionaries to work among the Goths. German mercenaries had been hired by Rome to maintain order in the eastern regions. Since the Goths had officially become part of the empire, mission work among them was easier.

Eventually, the Goths became missionaries to other German tribes—the Vandals, Suevi, Burgundians, Heruls, and others (249). One would imagine that with the introduction of Christianity the German societies would have begun the process of gradual change, internalizing Christian principles that would generate changes in values and behavior. Eventually such changes would occur. But for several centuries, Christianity was not sincerely embraced by the gothic people. Christian principles were not internalized and the changes that would normally follow a sincere conversion did not materialize. Cantor notes that the "Romanization" of the Germanic peoples, which included exposure to Christianity, seemed to have had little effect. Consequently, the Germans who eventually invaded the empire from across the Rhine were "fierce, ignorant and barbarian in every sense of the word" (1994:93).

90

This lack of change in the German culture, in spite of the presence of Christianity, becomes an important consideration in the larger issue of this study: understanding Western culture. Whatever impact Christianity may have in a given culture will be determined by how completely that culture will embrace and internalize Christian principles. A surface-level presence of Christianity (an outward, empty, ritualistic practice of Christian worship forms) does not make a people Christian. Faith in Christ that produces changes in how life is lived is what makes people (and societies) Christian.

Eventually, Christian principles were embraced and changes occurred in German society which signaled the presence of a genuine Christian faith. Generally, however, this did not occur until the Middle Ages. Sometimes it takes time for Christianity to have a significant impact. That reality has less to do with the nature of Christianity than with the nature of human beings who prefer to remain as they are.

The Fall of Rome

Christianity survived, the Empire did not. Why? Setting aside divine retribution and other theological considerations, there are a number of reasons the Empire began to falter. The actual fall or collapse of the empire is dated at 476. It was not an unexpected calamity, but a gradual process that ended in the inevitable. As to why this occurred, there has been much speculation. As I noted earlier, some blamed Christianity. Freeman notes that over the years there have been at least 500 theories that have attempted to explain the empire's demise (1996:519). Since other works have dealt with the subject exhaustively I will not duplicate that material. Instead, a brief summary from Will Durant will suffice:

91

[T]he fall of Rome. . . had not one cause but many, and was
not an event but a process spread over 300 years. Some nations
have not lasted as long as Rome fell.

A great civilization is not conquered from without until it
has destroyed itself within. The essential causes of Rome's
decline lay in her people, her morals, her class struggles, her
failing trade, her bureaucratic despotism, her stifling taxes, her
consuming wars (1944:665).

Along with these internal factors that weakened the
empire, were the external challenges along the eastern
borders. Near the end, Rome was unable to muster sufficient
forces to defend her borders and had to "outsource" the job
to German mercenaries, who eventually seized power in the
West, completing the collapse of the most powerful empire
the world had ever known.

The Greeks were gone, the Romans were gone.
Christianity was still there, a vital force in the life of a
struggling Western civilization.

Christianity in the Middle Ages

Great and glorious Rome was no more. The
barbarians had emerged victorious. Pieces of the once great
empire lay scattered across the forlorn European landscape
as shadowy clouds of chaos darkened the fragmented,
disheveled sea of humanity. Who or what would fill the void
left when the last vestiges of Roman influence faded from
view? The church. R. W. Southern observes that:

The fall of the Roman Empire left a mental and spiritual as
well as a political ruin which it took centuries to repair. The
collapse was a long and complicated business, but in the West it
was complete by the end of the seventh century. It was then
that the work of rebuilding began. The dominating ideal in the
rebuilding was that the unitary authority of the Empire should
be replaced by the unitary authority of the papacy. . . During the
whole medieval period there was in Rome a single spiritual and
temporal authority exercising powers which in the end exceeded

those that had ever lain within the grasp of a Roman Emperor, (1990:24-25).

Whether or not one appreciates the power the Roman church exercised during the medieval period is not the point. The point is the influence the church had on the development of Western culture. There can be little doubt that its influence was significant.

Christopher Dawson argues that it was the church (or Christianity) that stepped in after the collapse of Rome, providing the leadership and structure that allowed Western culture not only to survive, but to grow and change in dynamic ways. In some cases the church's influence was specific and direct. The church controlled land and resources and used those assets in ways that impacted society. In other cases the church's impact was more subtle, influencing the decisions of local rulers. Either way, Christianity's presence (in the form of the often wayward Catholic Church) in medieval Europe impacted not only that part of the world during that time, but has continued to impact the West and the entire world for over 1000 years (1950:15-25)[6].

What kinds of things occurred in the Middle Ages that allowed or caused Western culture to develop as it did? What did Christianity have to do with those developments? These are the questions that will be addressed in the following sections.

------

[6] No one who understands Christianity would argue that the Catholic church of the Middle Ages thought or acted in ways consistent with Christianity. There was, in those centuries, hypocrisy and brutality and theological foolishness that will forever shame and stain the reputation of Christianity. However, to acknowledge that all was not right is not to suggest that all was wrong. In the broad strokes and for the most part, Christianity during the Middle Ages was a vibrant positive spiritual force that held together and shaped in beneficial ways a society struggling with identity, meaning, and direction. There were shadows, but from among the shadows a great light emerged.

The Rise of the Submissive Ruler
with Limited Political Power

In 800, Pope Leo III crowned Charlemagne, proclaiming him Emperor of Rome, effectively creating what became the Holy Roman Empire, in which the church replaced the old Roman republic. There wasn't much left of the old empire by 800, but the coronation gave Charlemagne additional power and influence. He had been the king of the Franks since 768, one of many in a long line of Germanic barbarian rulers. The Germanic rulers had been "Christians" for centuries—at least in name. Christianity, however, had made little difference in the way they ruled (Mayr-Harting 2001:46-47). Charlemagne's reign, however, proved to be different. He took his responsibility seriously, seeing it as a sacred trust. His methods, which included forced conversions, were unfortunate, but his sincerity is admirable. He gathered scholars to his court and collected an impressive library. He also instituted studies of Latin so the Bible and "Christian culture" would be accessible. He made learning possible.

Charlemagne's focus on the importance of spiritual matters impacted all of Europe. By the end of his reign in 814, "medieval Europe was thoroughly Christian" (Collins and Price 2003:92). Even though this sociopolitical form of Christianity was not always the product of a sincere heartfelt conversion, the outward forms of Christian belief did impact the society in positive ways.

Beyond Charlemagne's general impact on European culture, the idea that kings and rulers should be humble, serving under God's rule and authority, can be traced back to him. Not that Charlemagne originated the idea. In the Old Testament, the kings of Israel and of other nations served their people as the servants of God, under his authority, by his laws. What made Charlemagne unique in his day was his willingness to accept this notion. His recognition of God's authority over his kingship stood in stark contrast to the arrogant presumption of the Roman Caesars and the pagan conquerors that had rampaged uncontrolled through the world for so many centuries. Charlemagne was familiar with the Hebrew Scriptures and saw himself as a "new David" (Mayr-Harting 1990:101). In addition to the clear message of the Old Testament, in the 590s, Pope Gregory the Great had written *Pastoral Care*, a book that stressed that the responsibility of rule was a stewardship from God (50). The point was not lost on Charlemagne.

The concept of the king being under the authority of God made it clear that the king did not have unlimited power. His power and authority were given to him by God and were, therefore, limited by God. The king could not simply do as he pleased—that is, if he respected and obeyed God. This meant that a godly king was a humble, obedient king.

Charlemagne's legacy of the humble ruler lives on in Western culture. Leadership is thought of as a sacred trust. Western rulers are subject not only to the will of God, but also to the will of the people.

The Rise of Monasticism

Historians who specialize in the Middle Ages are agreed that one of the major influences of the Middle Ages—an influence that shaped Western culture in significant ways—was the development of monasticism (Lawrence 2000:432), which Charlemagne encouraged during his reign. Dawson notes that:

> Any study of the origins of medieval culture must inevitably give an important place to the history of Western monasticism, since the monastery was the most typical cultural institution throughout the whole period that extends from the decline of the classical civilization to the rise of the European universities in the twelfth century—upwards of seven hundred

years. And it is even more important for the subject with which I am particularly concerned—the relation of religion and culture, for it was through monasticism that religion exercised a direct formative influence on the whole cultural development of these centuries (1950:44).

Cantor suggests that it was the combination of the papacy (the structure and leadership of the church) and the monks (the spiritual workforce that actually interacted with the people) that provided the strength to keep medieval European society from being crushed under the weight of barbarism. And of those two forces, Cantor notes, "it was the monks who were the most continuous force for education, organization, and social amelioration between the sixth and twelfth centuries and a determining factor of the most fundamental kind in the formation of medieval civilization" (1994:146).

Monasticism was not introduced or developed with these ends in mind. In fact, originally it was a life choice of extremists who were more influenced by second century Gnosticism than they realized. Monasticism was originally a form of asceticism, a rejection of all pleasure and enjoyment, an austere life of self-denial, often to the point of self-abuse. Ascetics often lived far into the desert, originally in North Africa—lonely hermits trying desperately to avoid the temptations of society.

More reasoned thinkers, however, such as Augustine, realized the folly of extremist responses. By the nature of their lifestyle, separatists cannot accomplish much that is useful in society. Eventually, thanks to the work of Augustine and others, the idea of monastic life came to be associated with "the ideal of the common life of the primitive church rather than by the intense asceticism of the monks of the desert" (Dawson 1950:47).

One of the earliest places where monasticism blossomed and began to impact society in a positive way was Ireland. The Irish monks were well educated and enthusiastic about their work. They were mission minded and led the way in converting Anglo-Saxons and reforming the church in Gaul. However, because the Irish church remained somewhat distant from Roman policy and authority, they were not able to sustain their influence. Eventually, Western monasticism became associated with the Benedictine order, so much so that the centuries between 550 and 1150 are often referred to as the Benedictine centuries (Cantor 149).

Western monasteries became self-contained, self-supporting, self-governing economic organisms. They were social and co-operative, a place of discipline (in the sense of training) for the common Christian life. They were considered "schools of the service of the Lord" (Dawson 48). They became places where capable men could sharpen their intellect and hone their skills for service to the Lord.

Generally speaking, the Middle Ages were a time of widespread illiteracy. Even some priests were illiterate. A few monasteries became places of Christian elementary education. As the idea caught on, educationally oriented Benedictine monasteries sprang up all over Europe, laying the foundation for a literate society. In time, as more people became literate, the level of education provided in the monastery rose and educated leaders began to emerge.

The task of education cannot be accomplished without books, without libraries. In addition to becoming schools, monasteries became places where books were produced. Monks copied manuscripts and bound them into books. Libraries were created.

Universities

At the same time learning was being rediscovered by society and facilitated by the monastic system, classic texts long forgotten in the West were being rediscovered. Aristotle was the major classical source to be rediscovered

97

and studied. His focus on studying nature, logic, and rhetoric supercharged an already intense educational atmosphere and provided the impetus that led to the formation of the first universities. By the beginning of the thirteenth century the universities of Paris, France and Bologna, Italy were the leading intellectual centers in Europe. Oxford was also gaining a reputation for expertise in the natural sciences.

The eleventh through the thirteenth centuries was a time of extraordinary growth in general. New cities sprang up; old cities experienced renewal and expansion (Le Goff 1988:70-80). As a result of the increased population, and fueled by favorable changes in weather patterns, crop production increased. Trade in goods increased, creating additional cash flow and capital. Building projects signaled expansion. Urban Europe was developing. A new way of living was being created. And along with new ways of urban living came new problems, new concerns, new questions that demanded new answers, new solutions, and new ways of thinking. The new universities served the intellectual and spiritual needs of the emerging new Europe quite nicely.

It must be remembered that the universities were a direct result of the monastic schools that had developed and served the intellectual and spiritual needs of Europe for five hundred years. The universities had grown out of Christian endeavors. They were staffed by Christians and were centers of Christian learning where church leaders, educators, philosophers, princes and kings were educated. Christianity was directly responsible for the development of the Western educational system that has benefited the world so thoroughly.

Hospitals

The monasteries also provided the original setting for medieval health care. From the earliest times, monasteries were places of hospitality and medical care. The Benedictine order was especially known for their concern for medical needs. They collected and studied ancient medical texts. During the various plagues that devastated Europe, monasteries served the needs of people suffering from bubonic plague, leprosy, small pox and other diseases.

One of the areas of specialization in the new universities was medicine. As Christianity gave rise to the university system of Western Europe, so, too it provided the foundation for the modern Western system of health care and its study in the universities. Monasteries, universities and hospitals are linked together as institutions of the Christian church.

This is not to say that Christianity invented education or health care. That is obviously not the case. The academies of Plato and Aristotle existed hundreds of years before Christianity, and advanced medical techniques were being practiced in Egypt and China long before the Christian era. But the question under consideration has to do with the features that shaped Western culture and Western people. Clearly, Western universities and Western hospitals are the direct descendants of medieval Christian monasticism.

Scholasticism

As I have already noted, part of the intellectual resurgence of the Middle Ages was the rediscovery of classical Greek philosophy, Aristotle's works being chief among them. As his works were translated into Latin they were read and re-read, discussed and argued. Aristotle's works became standard texts in the new universities. Europeans were learning from the Greeks to think about the world in new ways. What impact did the rediscovery of classic Greek philosophy have on the development of Western culture? Was Christianity a decisive factor in the integration of Aristotelian philosophy into the matrix of Western society?

Richard Rubenstein's work, *Aristotle's Children* (2003), chronicles the story of the loss and rediscovery of classical Greek philosophy in the West and its impact on the development of Western culture. Specifically, he points out that the struggle over what to do with ancient Greek philosophy occurred within the Christian community itself. And it was that struggle within the Christian community in the twelfth and thirteenth centuries that laid the foundation for the European Renaissance and Enlightenment.

> Imagine, more than four centuries before Francis Bacon and René Descartes proclaimed the Scientific Revolution, a recognizably modern perspective—rationalists, this-worldly, humanistic, and empirical—ignited cultural warfare throughout Western Europe, challenging traditional religious and social beliefs at their core. The struggle between faith and reason did not begin, as is so often supposed, with Copernicus's challenge to earth-centered cosmology or Galileo's trial by the Inquisition but with the controversy over Aristotle's ideas during the twelfth and thirteenth centuries. . . Surprisingly (at least for those trained to believe that the age of faith was an age of darkness), the decisive contest between rationalist and traditionalist thinking was not fought out in a confrontation between the medieval Church and its opponents. It took place within the Church, where forces favoring the new Aristotelian learning did battle with those opposing it (2003:5-6).

Jewish and Muslim scholars had rediscovered Greek philosophy centuries before. They had studied it and had already wrestled with the difficulties associated with the naturalistic, humanistic, rationalistic perspective characteristic of Aristotle's philosophy. A project to translate the ancient Greek manuscripts into Latin was underway in Toledo, Spain. It was there that medieval Christian theologians first came in contact with Aristotelian thinking.

100

As the translations were completed and Aristotle's work became available to scholars, a mixture of excitement and apprehension swept through the theological community. The question that had to be answered was: "Could Christian believers make sense of the universe, as Aristotle had attempted to do, and still remain believers?" (2003:84). How far were scholars willing to go in their quest to understand the world from a rational point of view? Was it possible to accept Aristotle's love of reason and his fascination of the natural world and its natural processes without accepting his pagan theology? Was it possible to integrate Greek philosophy and Christian theology without doing damage to Christian theology? Some theologians did not believe it was. Others were more optimistic. Among them were: Peter Abelard, Anselm of Canterbury, Thomas Aquinas, Duns Scotus, and Roger Bacon.

One of the earliest safeguards built into the attempted integration between theology and philosophy was the suggestion that where the two disciplines appeared to be in harmony both could be accepted. But where the two appeared to be in conflict theology must be the final arbiter of truth. The difficulty with this approach is one of perspective and opinion. One's perspective, the assumptions one holds when beginning an inquiry of any kind, including theological inquiries, have a great deal to do with the conclusion (opinion) one will reach as the inquiry is finalized. Evidently, this difficulty was not obvious to the medieval theologians who suggested it.

The integration of Aristotelian philosophy and medieval theology was an uneasy one to say the least. The academic interplay that emerged in the integration of the two disciplines and the subsequent comparison of what different scholars had to say on different subjects was later referred to as *scholasticism*—the comparing and contrasting views of accepted authorities. The philosopher-theologians who engaged in the process were referred to as scholastics.

101

A detailed analysis of scholasticism and the specific theological-philosophical issues that concerned Christian medieval scholars is beyond the scope of this brief study. However, as noted, the basic process of scholastic methodology was to compare and contrast views of accepted "authorities." Many detailed analyses of the process have already been completed and are available in other sources. My purpose is simply to expose the fact that the process of scholasticism, in comparing what various philosophers and theologians taught, was responsible for a change in thinking during the Middle Ages—which can be described as a major *paradigm shift*—and which made the Renaissance and Enlightenment possible. The people who were responsible for that paradigm shift were Christians. Their integration of Greek philosophy with medieval theology laid the intellectual foundation for significant changes yet to come. Medieval Christians changed the intellectual landscape of their day and in doing so changed the course of Western culture.

But to say that they laid the foundation for future changes is insufficient. They actually began the process. As Rubenstein points out, the "modern" scientific process is clearly visible in the work of the scholastics. Medieval scholastic scientists, such as Bruidan and Oresme, were making significant contributions to modern science long before the Renaissance began. Bruidan discovered a new way of thinking about motion, developing a formula that is "virtually the same as the modern formula for momentum" (275), and Oresme "arrived at a proof of the mean speed thermo that is substantially the same as that used by Galileo in the seventeenth century" (275).

During this "medieval renaissance" in the Middle Ages, Greek classical philosophy was rediscovered and integrated with theology to create new ways of thinking. It was in the Middle Ages that the failings of a number of Aristotleian assumptions were exposed, leading to the discovery of more accurate scientific perspectives. It was Christian scholastic scientists who began the "modernistic renaissance" movement away from Aristotleian thinking toward the more accurate scientific approach that characterized the historical period known as the Renaissance—a time when amazing progress was made. In reality it was Christian scholars who opened the door for the development of modern Western culture.

Summary

Empires rise, rule, diminish and disappear. Even the strongest age and atrophy and are carried away as dust in the wind. Such was the fate of Rome. Decay from within weakened her against attack from without. But as the power of Rome decreased, the influence of the church increased. It wasn't a perfect church by any stretch of the imagination. Anything that involves human beings is going to be imperfect. But the church's presence provided a cohesiveness, identity and direction that held a floundering civilization together.

Two key developments after the fall of Rome and through the Middle Ages where Christianity was the dominant influence were the rise of the submissive ruler with limited power, and the rise of monasticism. Each has impacted the West in significant ways. The concept of the submissive ruler is a hallmark of Western political leadership. And the educational and health care systems that developed within the framework of the monasteries have had a significant impact on the West as well. In fact, the West would not be the West it is were it not for these critical elements. To a large degree, Western culture and Western people are what they are because of the influence of Christianity in the Middle Ages.

103

Chapter 6

The Renaissance

"Between 1000 and 1500, Latin Christendom had doubled in size, and quadrupled in population," (Murray 2001:98). As the overall population of Europe increased so did the number of people living in cities. Le Goff notes that one of the most significant developments of the Middle Ages was the movement of much of the population from a rural to an urban setting. The development of cities changed the face of Europe (1988:74).

People thrust together in new urban settings create new problems that require new solutions. They raise new questions that require new answers. When the old ways no longer work, when the old perspectives no longer shed sufficient light, and the old worldview no longer provides a workable interpretation of reality, people will develop new ways of coping. A new or modified worldview will emerge.

In the thirteenth and fourteenth centuries, a series of crises created additional stress on social systems that were already strained. In common fashion, after a period of vast expansion, European economic growth ground to a halt and drifted into depression. Building programs were suspended. Even the great cathedrals sat unfinished. The population began to decline, which led to a further decline in trade.

There were strikes, urban uprisings, and revolts. Changes in weather patterns resulted in shorter growing seasons which diminished food production. People were hungry. In their weakened condition they were more vulnerable to sickness. When the Black Death (bubonic plague) swept through Europe in 1348, thirty to forty percent of the population died. Yet of this time Cantor notes:

> The crisis of the later Middle Ages did not distract the intellectuals and artists of Latin Christendom from theory and creativity. On the contrary, the gloom and doom of the times made them think all the more deeply about the nature of God, the universe, mankind, and society. In the midst of devastation from pandemics, war, climatic deterioration, and economic depression, they exhibited a passion for learning of all kinds— for linguistics and literary innovation, for philosophical and scientific inquiry, for massive productivity and creativity in the visual arts. No era in western civilization left a heritage of more masterpieces in literature and painting or seminal works of philosophy and theology (1993:529).

The era to which Cantor refers is known as the *Renaissance*, meaning the *rebirth*. This rebirth is generally considered to have begun in Northern Italy around 1300, extending eventually to the rest of Europe before coming to a close at the end of the 1500s. The Protestant Reformation was born in the last years of the Renaissance. Renaissance thinkers, though they did not specifically use the term Renaissance (Johnson 2002:3), thought of the times in which they lived as a time of rebirth because they believed they were emerging from the darkness of the past ages in a renewal of classical philosophy and learning that shed new light on what it meant to be human. However, a number of historians have demonstrated that the *dark ages* were not as dark as some, especially Renaissance thinkers themselves, imagined. Rubenstein (2003) has demonstrated that the Middle Ages were an exciting time of discovery and growth. It is accurate to say, though, that the discovery and growth that began in the Middle Ages continued and intensified, often in quantum leaps, during the Renaissance.

Renaissance Culture

My purpose in this brief overview is to highlight a few of the significant people, perspectives, and developments in European culture during the Renaissance and then consider the impact those things had and continue to have on Western culture in general. It is important to remember that the largest percentage of the population in Europe during the Renaissance was Christian. They may not have been thoroughly knowledgeable, committed Christians, but they were believers. God, Jesus, sin, moral absolutes, prayer, forgiveness, salvation: these were ideas they embraced.

Intellectual Culture

The intellectual culture of the renaissance can be described as humanistic, scientific, and individualistic.

Humanistic

Three names regularly associated with the early stages of Renaissance humanism are Dante, Boccaccio, and Petrarch. Humanism, as it existed during the Renaissance, had to do with "an educational and cultural program based on the study of the classics and colored by the notion of human dignity implicit in *humanitas*" (Rice and Grafton 1994:78). The "*human dignity* implicit in the *humanitas*" had to do with a view of humans as rational beings created in God's image, capable of discovering truth and living good lives.

Humanists stressed the importance of civic responsibility, of being socially aware and active, of

106

participating in the political life of the community. Renaissance humanism was a *Christian humanism* rooted not in human depravity (a theological perspective espoused by Augustine), but in human dignity, free will, rationality, and the ability to excel and succeed, to grow and become. It is important to understand the difference between Renaissance Christian humanism and the later forms of secular humanism often associated with an anti-God or anti-Christian philosophical perspective. It is also important to understand how fundamental this view—a view of humans as rational beings created in God's image, capable of discovering truth and living good lives—is as a worldview assumption of Western people about the nature of humanity. There are a few theological traditions that would differ with this perspective on the nature of man, agreeing with Augustine that humanity is depraved. However, this Christian humanistic perspective regarding the nature of humanity has been a fundamental feature of the predominant Western worldview.

Dante is considered by many to be the greatest of the Renaissance thinkers (Johnson 2002:25). His *Divine Comedy*, a story describing his trip through hell, purgatory and heaven, was intended to provide moral instruction regarding the kinds of behavior that result in punishment versus reward. One of the themes of the epic poem has to do with the achieving of inner peace through the use of reason and love. It was popular among all classes of people and focused attention on the importance of individual behavior, inspiring readers to think differently about themselves and about life.

The works of Boccaccio, a poet and novelist, and of Petrarch, a lyricist, may not be as well known as Dante's. But their stories, poems and songs of love, tragedy, or triumph deeply rooted in the human experience, focused on humanity rather than divinity, provided additional impetus for the humanistic focus of that time, a focus on individuality and rationality, key features of the Western view of personhood.

Scientific

The Renaissance can be characterized as a time of significant scientific progress. Renaissance thinkers were able to build on the foundation laid by scientists in the Middle Ages after the rediscovery of classical science. One example of the far-reaching impact of Renaissance science is Copernicus and his work in astronomy. In 1543, building on the work of the ancient astronomer Ptolemy and others, Copernicus published *De Revolutionibus Orbium Caelestium*, in which he suggested a heliocentric (sun-centered) rather than a geocentric (earth-centered) solar system. Copernicus' work was very narrow and extremely technical. Only those well versed in the science of astronomy could follow it. Copernicus did not claim to have discovered or even rediscovered that the earth moved around the sun. In his preface he gives credit to ancient astronomers who suggested the possibility long before he had. Yet it was the presentation of his work (in just the right way at just the right time) that resulted in what is now referred to as the *Copernican Revolution* (Kuhn 1985:134-144).

Thomas Kuhn notes that while the name of the revolution is singular, the event itself was plural, transforming thinking not only in the field of mathematical astronomy, but also resulting in "conceptual changes in cosmology, physics, philosophy and religion as well." From Copernicus' work "men were able to create a new physics, a new conception of space, and a new idea of man's relation to God," (1985:vii).

Not all Renaissance science impacted the development of Western culture as did the work of Copernicus. Still, it was a time of experimentation and discovery that freed people from the limitations of unfounded assumptions, allowing curious, progressive thinkers to forge ahead into uncharted territory, blazing a scientific trail that is still being followed today. Their work, however, was not fully appreciated and did not go unchallenged. The *status quo* is a cherished commodity not easily relinquished. Many church officials, whose thought processes were still enslaved to tradition and superstition, vigorously opposed any idea they perceived to be a threat to long established orthodox dogma. It is important to note that such conflicts took place between Christians with differing perspectives, not between believers and unbelievers. Fortunately, most forward thinking Christians would not be silenced by their frightened counterparts. Scientific minded people (who were Christian people) forged ahead, leading the western world into new ways of thinking about and studying the world. They were demonstrating that it was possible to believe in God and still, as the Greeks had done, study the world naturalistically. Renaissance science laid the foundation for a way of thinking that was naturalistic and rationalistic (scientific) and yet rooted in an overarching supernaturalistic perspective where God was present and welcome.

Individualistic

One of the most unique characteristics of Western culture is its individualistic orientation. The seeds of Western individualism were planted by the Greeks. The seeds sprouted and were nurtured in the Middle Ages. During the Renaissance the flower of individualism blossomed.

Living conditions during the feudal period of Europe's development (in the Middle Ages) did not offer opportunities for individual solitude. Overcrowding thrust people together in uneasy proximity. Beyond those physical considerations, the intellectual climate did not lend itself to individualistic thought or behavior. Individualism was discouraged in the eleventh and twelfth centuries. Behavior that separated one from the group placed the separated individual at risk, not only from those not part of one's group (robbers, for instance) but from the members of one's own (prior) group. Conform or suffer serious consequences was the clear message.

Yet even in an atmosphere that stifled individualistic response, evidence exists that demonstrates the presence of incipient individualism. As land was cleared and became available, people relocated to create new and better opportunities for themselves. The idea of personal property that needed to be safeguarded became more of an issue as people began utilizing locks with keys to secure their property. (Private property and individualism go hand in hand.) As business opportunities became available, making private wealth possible, greater value was placed on personal initiative. The value of the individual increased.

Even in monasteries, monks were given *private time* to pursue individual devotional interests. Christians were encouraged to struggle with the spiritual forces of evil as individuals. One could be part of a group (family or church) and still retain his or her individual personality and perspective (Duby 1988:509-533).

During the Renaissance itself, in the fourteenth and fifteenth centuries, one of the most telling evidences of the presence of individualism was the rising popularity of the portrait. In earlier times, painters mostly painted thematic representations related to spiritual concerns. But as the Renaissance evolved more and more painters selected individuals as their subjects. Or, through the use of perspective, individuals were singled out to serve as the central focus of a painting (Braunstein 1988:556-561).

The rise of subjectivism (an individual or personal perspective) during the Renaissance also signals the rise of individualism. Philippe Braunstein observes that:

110

> Social life comprises a series of communities: family, traditional community, professional groups, subjects of a sovereign. The individual is more than a member of so many different groups. Self-consciousness is born when the individual can see himself in perspective, set apart from his fellow man; it can lead to a radical questioning of the social order (1988:536).

As people began to perceive of themselves not only in relation to a group (family, church, business, etc.) but as unique "self-conscious" individuals, what he or she thinks suddenly matters. Linguistic use of the first person singular began to increase. Slowly, the art of autobiographical narrative developed, allowing individuals to express their uniqueness in a direct and specific way. The importance of community was not lost in the Renaissance, but the importance of the individual began to supersede the importance of the community. The precious Western view that the person is first and foremost an individual and only secondarily a member of a community, came to fruition during the Renaissance.

Material Culture

The way a people think, their view of themselves and of their world, is part of their intellectual culture. Understanding the intellectual culture of a people is crucial to understanding their material culture, that is, how they structure their society for daily living—their surface-level culture. A complete detailed analysis of daily life during the Renaissance is beyond the scope of this brief study. But three areas of daily life during the Renaissance will provide some examples to be examined: economics, politics, art.

Economics

Economics is a broad and complicated category. Rather than attempting to discuss it in detail it may be more effective to introduce a basic concept and then illustrate it with an example. As the feudalism of the eleventh century began to decompose, capitalism began to emerge. Though Roberts suggests a later date—the 18th century (2000:94), it is during the Renaissance that the early stages of a capitalistic system are clearly recognizable.

Michel Beaud believes that "capitalism is above all a complex social logic able to transform the world around it at the same time it is able to transform itself" (2001:6). His point is that there is more to capitalism than technical economic considerations. Typically, capitalism is thought of as an economic system. The means of production are privately owned (by individuals or corporations rather than the government) and that which is produced, and the income that results, is distributed largely through the operation of markets, that is, supply and demand. This may be an accurate definition of capitalism, but Beaud would likely suggest that it does not do justice to the complexity and pervasiveness of capitalism.

The development of the printing industry during the Renaissance provides an example of how capitalism evolved during that time. A German named Johannes Gutenberg is credited with inventing the Western style process of printing with movable metal type, around 1450 in Mainz, Germany. The frame for the press was wood. The type itself was metal. An oil based ink was used to print on paper. The development of the oil based ink used in printing can be traced to Flemish artists who used oil based paints in their work. The manufacture of paper suitable for printing began in Spain and slowly made its way into Europe (Rice and Grafton 1994:1-7). The manufacture or availability of wood,

112

metal, ink, paper and more were all necessary for the printing industry to develop.

The availability of necessary collateral material allowed for the development of the new printing industry. There also had to be a need, that is, a market. There was a market because of the emphasis the scholastics had placed on education. Because of the universities developed in the Middle Ages, greater numbers of people were literate and desirous of material to read. But before something can be printed it must be written. If there is a writer there must also be an editor, a publisher, a typesetter, a book binder, and a book seller. Whatever else may be said about capitalism, clearly, as the development of the publishing industry illustrates, it is a collaborative effort.

According to Rice and Grafton, printing within Germany and Austria spread from Mainz to Strasbourg, Cologne, Augsburg, Nuremberg, Leipzig, and Vienna. Then to other regions, including: Italy, Switzerland, Bohemia, France, the Netherlands, Denmark and Sweden. Within fifty years, six million books had been printed (1994:7).

In each case, printing shops were private enterprises. The business owner provided the capital to start and run the business. Paper and ink suppliers had to be paid. Wages had to be paid. Product had to be sold. The cost of supplies and labor as well as market demand had to be factored into the selling price. A percentage of the profit was reinvested back into the business to improve or expand manufacturing and to expand markets. All of this was accomplished in the private sector. Capital for investment, a market for the product, and the freedom to risk and succeed is what drove the system.

There was a market for books because there were educated people who wanted books to read. The production of vast quantities of books allowed for the development of extensive library collections which meant that even more people would have access to books and the higher levels of education they made possible. Universities would be able to serve the needs of more students. As more books were produced the cost per book was reduced, making them less expensive. The average person could afford to buy books. The availability of books changed European society. Typography was probably the single greatest invention of the Renaissance (Rice and Grafton 1994:5).

Imagine the pervasive impact of the printing industry on Renaissance society multiplied ten times as other industries developed and expanded. Multiply that ten more times and ten more times. In a sense, everything becomes connected to everything else as the system itself evolves exponentially. The results are staggering. This is what Beaud meant when he spoke of capitalism as "a complex social logic able to transform the world around it at the same time it is able to transform itself."

Did Christianity play a part in the development of capitalism? Yes it did. The question is, how big a part? Arriving at a definitive answer may be difficult. At the very least it can be said that Christianity was indirectly involved in the development of Western capitalism because the people who created it were Christian people. They were educated in the university system created by the scholastics and run by their spiritual descendants. Enlightened by a classical Christian education that had resulted in the development of Christian humanism, progressive thinking entrepreneurs saw new ways of taking advantage of new opportunities. Capitalism was the economic result of a larger Renaissance perspective (an evolving worldview) that was possible because of the medieval rediscovery and Christian reinterpretation of classical (Greek) thinking.

It is important, however, to stress that while the role of Christianity in the development of capitalism may be considered by some as merely *indirect*, others, such as Max Weber (1958) and R. H. Tawney (1954), have argued that the role of Christianity in the development of Western economic practices was fundamental, far-reaching and crucial. Some may feel that Weber and Tawney have overstated their case. The degree to which Christianity is responsible for the development of Western capitalism may never be agreed on by experts in the field. However, it can be said that of the many factors merged simultaneously to make capitalism possible, one of them was Christianity. If nothing else, Christianity provided the basic ethical foundation necessary to sustain successful, profitable business relations. While it would be insupportable in the minds of some to claim a more decisive role for Christianity in the development of capitalism, it is foolish to ignore or deny its influence in the evolution of the economic process.

The importance of capitalism in the development of Western culture cannot be overestimated. If there is a feature of Western culture that comes to mind right alongside democracy, it is capitalism. And while capitalism cannot be classified as Greek or Christian, elements of both perspectives must be present for capitalism to flourish: the individual freedom to risk and excel that is usually associated with democracy, and a basic moral and ethical environment of honesty and trustworthiness that is usually associated with Christianity.

Politics

Christian values and thinking did not provide the foundation for all the cultural changes and developments that occurred during the Renaissance. One example of this is the development of new and more effective methods of warfare. "In no period before our own has the technology of violence been more fertile than in the century between 1450 and 1550. During these years the use of gunpowder to propel missiles transformed the art of war" (Rice and Grafton 1994:10-11). The presence of guns in Europe probably dates back to the early 1300s. By the end of that century firearms were being manufactured all over Europe. Castle strongholds that had proven so effective against medieval methods of warfare were vulnerable to canon fire. So, too, the armor knights had worn in battle for protection against swords and arrows proved vulnerable to rifle and pistol shots.

New weapons gave rise to new military strategies and new methods of dealing with conflict. Along with these changes in methodology came complementary changes in ideology. Personal and political loyalties in medieval times were prioritized first spiritually, then materially. God came first. (At least this was the claim. Whether or not it was actually true remains open to debate.) Then came loyalty to a local lord or one's village. During the late medieval period, however, kings began cultivating a spirit of nationalism or patriotism—loyalty to country and king, an affinity for others like oneself, those who speak the same language (Spickard and Cragg 1994:163). The political power of the church had been diminished drastically and local nobles eventually understood that they could not compete with the energizing, organizing power of a national monarch determined to consolidate his power. An army funded at the national level armed with massive firepower was a force to be reckoned with. So was the king that commanded such a weapon.

It is difficult to imagine a link between the technology and politics of Renaissance warfare and Christianity. Those negative realities developed in spite of the presence and influence of Christianity. If there is an upside to the deadly political conflicts of the Renaissance (for instance the 1525 battle of Pavia between the French and Spanish for control of northern Italy) perhaps it is that the presence of Christianity may have prevented the new weaponry, wielded in the name of nationalistic interests, from being used in even more brutal ways than it was.

Art

Artistic expression during the Renaissance paralleled the philosophic thinking of that time. The humanistic focus that had begun with the scholastics and their rediscovery of classical philosophy intensified during the Renaissance. It wasn't that people were no longer interested in God or spiritual realities. They were. But they began to see that as rational people living in a rational, predictable world, they could understand the material creation better, which included humanity, if they focused greater attention on it. They could make life better if they paid attention to it, studied it, and manipulated it. This intense focus on life lived in a material world was expressed most eloquently in the Renaissance arts: literature, sculpture, painting and music. A detailed analysis of each of these categories is beyond the scope of this brief study. A few observations regarding Renaissance painting, however, will serve to illustrate the nature of Renaissance art.

Painting in the Middle Ages was flat, two dimensional. It was almost entirely religious in nature. Biblical scenes or Christian personalities were represented in static disproportionate styles, often painted on gold foil in unrealistic colors meant to suggest an *other-worldly* context or orientation. But with the dawn of the Renaissance and a philosophical reorientation that focused more attention on the real world, painters sought to represent earthly realities in a realistic manner. Science and art merged as artists began using mathematics to calculate perspective, experimenting with techniques and devices (frames through which they viewed subjects) designed to assist them in producing paintings that were windows on the world.

Along with new styles of presentation, the subject matter of Renaissance art changed dramatically. Religious subjects were still a significant focus of Renaissance art, especially of the early Renaissance. But alongside the

117

religious art came representations of everyday life in the material world. Artists who looked at the world from a new humanist perspective saw dozens of new subjects to paint. Landscapes were of special interest. Careful attention was given to the presentation of trees and plants, especially flowers. Mountains, streams, rivers, and cloud-filled skies gained prominence. So did people—people doing everyday mundane things. The body itself became a focus of Renaissance art. Since God had taken a human form in the incarnation, Petrarch had reasoned, he placed his stamp of approval on it. The human body was nothing to be ashamed of. Rather, it should be appreciated and celebrated. Renaissance artists experimented with nudity, even in religious paintings. The people in them were portrayed as real people living real life in a real world. Since the body was part of life in the real world it did not need to be covered anymore than a tree or a flower needed to be covered.

One of the goals of Renaissance painting was to present a representation that was as realistic as possible. Subject, perspective, proportion, color, shape, detail, placement, texture: attention to these and other details allowed the overall composition to reflect reality in ways unavailable in previous ages. In a way, Renaissance painters attempted to do with paint and brush something akin to what a photographer today might do—capture reality. Much of what they attempted to capture was historical scenes of religious or spiritual significance (something a photographer cannot do) but they attempted to make them as *real-world* as they could.

What role did Christianity play in Renaissance art? A very significant role. All one has to do to understand the role of Christianity on Renaissance art is to flip through a book of Renaissance art. Painting after painting after painting represents some event of spiritual significance. Christian humanists were vitally interested in humanity and the material world. That did not mean, however, that they

118

were not interested in spiritual realities. They were sincere, dedicated believers who took their faith seriously. But they were also humanists who took their humanity seriously. God had created humans and put them in the physical world, giving them the responsibility of managing it. How could they manage it effectively without studying and understanding it?

I am not suggesting that this was the exact reasoning of the Renaissance humanists. But I am suggesting that whether or not they fully realized their managerial responsibilities, their focus on understanding and managing life in the material world was right and good. They were very interested in living their Christian faith in the context of a real world. They were attempting to contextualize their faith to the world they lived in. The subject matter and style of presentation in Renaissance art makes this clear.

Christianity During the Renaissance

First, in considering Christianity during the Renaissance it is essential to remember that Christianity and the Catholic Church are not one and the same. Christianity as a spiritual reality, an internalized faith expressed in the day-to-day lives of individual believers, must not be so linked with the ecclesiastical hierarchy of the papacy that one cannot be distinguished from the other. *The Church* during the Renaissance and *Christianity* during the Renaissance are not the same things.

Second, in considering Christianity during the Renaissance it is essential to understand that the clergy and dogmatic traditionalists were not representative of all believers. There were dedicated Christians during the Renaissance who were not afraid to think differently, not afraid to express their faith from a new perspective—a Christian humanistic perspective.

What has this got to do with the development of Western culture? It is the blending and contrasting of Christian thought with the philosophy that began to emerge in the Renaissance that created the modern Western worldview, the foundation of Western culture. So understanding the way Christianity blended with philosophy during the Renaissance is crucial to understanding the development of Western, and therefore American, culture.

Progressive Thinkers

Often, when historians speak of the conflicts between the church and humanists of the Renaissance, they leave the impression that Renaissance humanists were not Christians. Most of the humanist thinkers of the Renaissance were not priests, but that does not mean that they were *secular*, that is, having nothing to do with religion. Renaissance humanists were not dogmatic traditionalists afraid to approach reality from a different perspective. They were progressive Christian thinkers willing to lay aside untested assumptions of traditional theological interpretations and analyze the world and physical life from a new perspective. This put them at odds with traditionalists within the church who had come to believe that their view of things represented the single, correct view of reality. As far as those traditionalists were concerned, views or explanations different from their own had to be wrong. Progressive thinkers represented a challenge to the *status quo*, a danger to the cherished orthodoxy of the traditionalists.

One of the most annoying habits of progressive thinkers is the way they seem to ask questions about everything, challenging the most fundamental assumptions. This is what had begun with the rediscovery of classical philosophy. But it seemed to reach new heights in the Renaissance. Progressive Renaissance thinkers questioned attitudes toward the body, expressed in the nudity that was

120

the subject of much of their art. They questioned theological traditions that were rooted in unchallenged presuppositions, such as the earth being the center of the solar system. They questioned the authority of the church to provide an official interpretation of Scripture rather than allowing individuals to interpret the Scriptures for themselves.

They questioned economic structures, political structures, philosophical structures, theological structures— nothing was sacred to the progressive thinkers of the Renaissance. Everything was open to investigation and reinterpretation. This is what set the orthodox traditionalists on edge. Nothing was sacred to the progressives. To the traditionalists, the progressives were a menace. But again it is important to note that the conflicts of the Renaissance were not between believers and unbelievers, as Rubenstein has demonstrated. The conflicts were between traditionalist and progressive Christians. Christians who wanted to understand the world God had created were studying it and relating to it in new ways, unfettered by the assumptions of previous ages.

The foundation for the modern Western worldview was laid by progressive thinking Christians. The doors of modern scientific investigation opened by progressive Renaissance thinkers were, in reality, opened by Christians. This is not to suggest that everything about the modern Western worldview was or is Christian. That is certainly not the case. Neither is it to suggest that everything that developed in Western culture was or is Christian and pleasing to God. It was not. The point is that the forward thinking people of the Renaissance were people of faith who saw no contradiction between their new perspective and their Christian faith.

Renaissance and Religious Reformation

The new philosophical and theological paradigms of the Renaissance are nowhere more evident than in the charges made against the Catholic church regarding its theological and moral abuses. Martin Luther led the way when in 1517 he nailed his ninety-five complaints to the door of the church in Wittenberg, Germany. Luther believed that the Scriptures alone should govern people's lives and the life of a congregation of believers. The Catholic officials, as far as Luther was concerned, had no authority to dictate in matters of faith.

While Luther was a fierce opponent of Aristotle and the scholastics of the Late Middle Ages, he was a product of Renaissance culture. The theological/philosophical paradigm from which he worked was antiauthoritarian and individualistic, perspectives that can be traced to ancient Greece, that were lost and rediscovered in the late Middle Ages, and that continued to evolve throughout the Renaissance. In other words, the religious reformation of the renaissance was possible because of the changes in thinking that characterized the Renaissance. People were willing to question authority. They were willing to think about things from a new point of view. They had experienced dramatic change in so many other areas of life that they were ready for a change in matters related to faith and religion as well.

The Christian humanism of the Renaissance was rooted in a developing individualism and a willingness to challenge the *status quo*. It permeated nearly every area of life, including religion. The Reformation was possible because of Renaissance humanism. Within that broad context, Christianity was a living, dynamic force involved in shaping culture in significant ways. People of faith were willing to rebel against long established cultural standards. And they were willing to rebel based on their personal assessment of the way things were versus the way they

122

believed things ought to be. Their rebellion demonstrated not only the power of the new spirit of individualism but also the power of deeply held religious convictions. So powerful were their convictions and the subsequent challenge to ecclesiastical authority that it led to a complete restructuring of church and society. That so many Europeans could rise up in rebellion against the moral and theological abuses of the Catholic church, the most powerful entity of that day, signaled a will and determination of the people to engage in a form of religious democracy that would, in a few hundred years, be expressed in the form of political democracy.

How significant was the Reformation in the development of Western culture? Thomas Carlyle, a Scottish essayist and historian, suggested that had Martin Luther not stood his ground there would have been no French Revolution and no America (Collinson 2000:601-602). Some may suggest this may be something of an overstatement on Carlyle's part, but it does reflect the enormous significance attached to the Reformation by historians. All of Western culture was impacted by the Reformation: religion, politics, economics, education, and so forth. The West is the West it is today (especially America) because of the Reformation. And the Reformation occurred because people of faith took their faith seriously. It is not an exaggeration to say that Christianity is a foundational feature of Western culture.

Summary

The Renaissance was a time of rebirth. Classical philosophy had been rediscovered and studied and the impact was beginning to be felt. People could be Christians and still think about the world from a natural, rational point of view. All of creation could be investigated and understood. Experimentation, exploration, and enterprise characterized European society during the Renaissance.

The view of human beings as rational beings, created in God's image, capable of discovering truth and living good lives fueled a new passion for discovery and achievement. This Christian humanism, generating new levels of individualistic expression, allowed progressive thinkers to excel scientifically, economically, politically and artistically in ways not even the Greeks had imagined.

There was tension during the Renaissance between the traditionalist Christian thinkers and the progressive thinkers (many of whom were Christians) just as there had been in the Middle Ages. Fortunately the progressive thinks would not be quieted. They would not be stopped. And the world, including Christianity, is better for it.

I'm not suggesting that Christianity as a belief drove the Renaissance. I'm not suggesting that the Renaissance happened as a result of Christian belief. Greek philosophy had more to do with the spirit of inquiry and progress during the Renaissance than Christianity. What I'm suggesting is that many (though not all) of the progressive thinkers who led the Renaissance were people of faith, people who believed in God, Jesus, moral absolutes, sin, forgiveness, and salvation. They were people who understood that one could be a person of faith and a person of science. While the science evolved out of a Greek perspective, the moral and ethical framework for the progress that was made grew out of the Judeo-Christian tradition that, at that time, still held sway. The presence of Christianity in Europe during the Renaissance was, as it had been for centuries, a significant and formative presence.

The religious Reformation that occurred near the end of the Renaissance was a powerful testimony to the need (which the Greeks had understood) for the freedom to think critically and analytically about all areas of life, including religion. That so many Europeans could rise up in rebellion against the moral and theological abuses of the Catholic church, the most powerful entity of that day, signaled a will and determination of the people to engage in a form of religious democracy that would, in a few hundred years, be expressed in the form of political democracy.

Indeed, the Renaissance was a crucial time of rebirth. The rebellious spirit of human independence and individualism that enlivened the ancient Greeks was reborn and in turn gave birth to a spirit of discovery and invention and a longing for freedom that in time would change not only the West but eventually the world.

Chapter 7

The Enlightenment

The amazing era of exploration, experimentation and enterprise that characterized the Renaissance wound down and came to a close by the end of the sixteenth century. Most historians date the beginning of the Enlightenment near the end of the seventeenth century, around 1680 (Kramnick 1995:x). During the later part of the Renaissance, and in the intervening years before the beginning of the one hundred or so years referred to as the *Enlightenment*, a number of people made scientific and philosophical contributions that impacted Western culture in significant ways, laying the foundation for Enlightenment thinking.

Pre-Enlightenment Philosophy

A number of historians focus their attention on three people who played key roles in the scientific and philosophical thinking that bridged the gap between the Renaissance and the Enlightenment: Bacon, Descartes, and Spinoza. A brief overview of each of these significant thinkers may be helpful.

Francis Bacon

Bacon (1561-1626) was a philosopher who devoted himself to converting people from the limitations of scholastic methodology (comparing and contrasting views of accepted authorities) to a scientific, rationalistic method of inquiry. Only through the application of reason could humanity hope to understand and control the laws of nature. According to Frost, Bacon was a proponent of the complete separation of religion and philosophy, arguing that "the doctrines of religion could not be proved by thinking and that men should give up the attempt," (1962:29). Bacon's goal was to "develop a method of thinking which would give mankind true knowledge about his universe," (29-30). Using an inductive method, Bacon was sure that humans could discover the laws and causes of the universe.

For humans to free themselves of the hindrances that stood in the way of such knowledge, Bacon perceived that humans would have to banish a number of "idols" (ideas) from their thinking. These idols were 1) *idols of the tribe*, 2) *idols of the den*, 3) *idols of the marketplace*, and 4) *idols of the theater*. What did Bacon mean?

Idols of the tribe had to do with ideas or behaviors that were common to all people—the human tribe. Specifically, it is normal for people to think that what they perceive is a direct and accurate reflection of reality. People fail to realize that sense perceptions are at least partially dependent of the human mind for classification and interpretation and are, therefore, relative in nature. Like a piece of highly polished but curved metal, sense perceptions present a distorted reflection of reality. Bacon believed that the world could be understood better if people realized their sense perceptions were relative (Cranston 1967: Vol. 1, 237).

Idols of the den had to do with Bacon's view of Plato's cave illustration. In Plato's cave, people in the cave saw shadowy reflections on the cave wall and mistook them for reality. Bacon felt that Plato's illustration was not personal enough, that each person (not humanity or society in general, but each person) had his or her own den from which he or she viewed and interpreted life. The resulting *personal perspective* was flawed because not only is it a sense perception of reality, it is a personal sense perception of realty filtered through that individual's personal perspective (238). Idols of the tribe and idols of the den are closely related.

Idols of the marketplace had to do with the challenges of the imprecise use of language in day-to-day activities such as commerce. People talk with one another, using words differently without realizing it and without understanding the level of miscommunication that is occurring. Bacon also noted that people have a tendency to confuse the names given to things with the things themselves. Our typical use of linguistic symbols is as imprecise for discussing reality as are our senses in perceiving reality (238). Bacon felt that people needed to be aware of the imprecise nature of communication and strive for greater precision.

Idols of the theater had to do with mistaken conclusions that people reach due to flawed philosophical systems. For Bacon, flawed philosophy would include Plato, who, according to Bacon, confused philosophy and theology, or systems that, on the one hand, make everything dependent on experience, or on the other, completely eliminate experience from the philosophical equation (238).

Bacon felt that these "idols" (mistaken assumptions) had to be eliminated and replaced by an enlightened rationalistic approach. He advocated an inductive, empirical approach, which meant that a statement or proposition is considered to be true when one's experience verifies its truthfulness.

Bacon was one of the early proponents of reason as humanity's hope for progress. Subsequent philosophers may have approached the subject from different perspectives, but Bacon's work was foundational for Enlightenment thinkers.

René Descartes

Descartes, a devout Christian (1596-1650), is considered by many to be the father of modern philosophy. He believed that the physical world could be explained by the use of mathematical and scientific principles. Before Descartes (and Bacon), philosophy had been rooted in the Scholastic approach of comparing and contrasting the views of recognized authorities—Plato believed one thing while Aristotle believed another. Descartes, however, preferred a rational inductive method, beginning with that which was beyond doubt. There had to be a place to begin, not an assumption, but a rationally verifiable truth or reality. From there, one could use reason to extrapolate and conclude. For Descartes, the place to begin was with himself. For him, the reality of his existence was his indisputable truth, his beginning point. He expressed this truth in his datum: *Cogito, ergo sum*, I think, therefore I am. Descartes knew he was real. His own existence was his verifiable reality.

From this beginning point Descartes proceeded to construct what is known as the *Cartesian* system. Mind, intellect or rationale must be allowed to work independently of the senses and emotions because senses and emotions can be deceived, leading one to false conclusions (as in Bacon's *idols of the tribe* and *idols of the den*). Descartes believed that humans were born with innate ideas in the mind and that those preexisting ideas outweighed the experiences of life. That which one concluded rationally, having begun with an indisputable fact, could be trusted. That which came of experience could not be trusted (Williams 1967: Vol. 2, 344-354).

It is important to note that both Bacon and Descartes were Christian humanists who emphasized the importance of reason. Bacon was an (early) empiricist, stressing the value of experience as a method of verification, while Descartes was a rationalist who preferred reason over experience. Reason was Descartes' method of verification, the source of justifiable knowledge. Rationalist and empiricist approaches to philosophy were advocated throughout the Enlightenment. British philosophers such as Bacon tended toward empiricism, French and German philosophers tended toward the rationalism of Descartes and those who followed him.

Descartes viewed people as *autonomous rational beings* (individuals) capable of using reason to understand the world and control their fate. Many people see Descartes' focus on humans as autonomous rational beings as the identifiable beginning of the individualistic orientation that is characteristic of the modern Western worldview. However, we have seen that the Western individual orientation can be traced all the way back to ancient Greece. Descartes' views, though different from Bacon's were, like Bacon's, foundational to Enlightenment thinking.

Baruch Spinoza

Spinoza was Jewish, born in Amsterdam, Holland (1632). In 1656 he withdrew from the Jewish community over philosophical and political differences. Spinoza believed in God, but not the personal God of the Scriptures. His view of God was rooted in pantheism. The universe was indivisible and God was everything. For Spinoza, an ethical life involved self-preservation, and friendship. Each of these was to be governed by the exercise of reason. Politically, he believed that since people must be free to pursue self-preservation, the government's power over them must be limited. Kenny points out that in Spinoza's "theologico-political treatise, (Tractatus Theologico-Poltitcus)," he "presented a political theory which, starting from a Hobbes-like view of human beings in a state of nature, derived thence the necessity of democratic government, freedom of speech, and religious toleration," (1998: 220).

Spinoza was a thorough-going rationalist, agreeing with Descartes, fundamentally, that one had to begin with self-evident truths and reason one's way forward. He did, however, believe Descartes to be wrong on a number of points (Brown 1990: 185-186). His work was not as influential as Bacon's or Descartes', but his conclusions regarding the limited power of government are part of the larger picture of pre- or early Enlightenment thinking that helped shape the thinking of later Enlightenment philosophers. The pre-enlightenment focus on the importance of reason in humanistic endeavors became the overarching concept of the Enlightenment.

Enlightenment Philosophy

Immanuel Kant's essay, *What is the Enlightenment?* contains perhaps the most concise comment that captures the nature of Enlightenment philosophy. It is his phrase, *dare to think*. Kant's point was that human beings should use their rational abilities to think for themselves. The emphasis of the Enlightenment was on the utilization of human reason to study humanity and the material world in order to discover ultimate truths about humanity and the world.

Enlightenment belief in the power of human rationality, and the implications of that rationality, was rooted in three basic assumptions: 1) that all humans are rational people, 2) that individuals have the right to live according to the dictates of their reason, and 3) that through the use of reason ultimate truth could be discovered (Brittan 1999:266).

The foundation for such thinking was laid during the Middle Ages with the rediscovery of classical philosophy. Renaissance thinkers, who were Christian humanists, built on that foundation, cultivating and elevating reason with their scientific and humanistic inquiries. Post-Renaissance philosophers, such as Bacon, Descartes, Spinoza, and others, continued the process, refining it, elevating human reason to new heights. Newton's discovery of the law of universal gravitation convinced people that if human reason could unlock the laws of the universe (the very laws of God) then nothing was beyond the reach of human reason. Using reason, humans could unlock the remaining secrets of the universe and solve the problems of humanity, achieving perfection as rational beings. This became to goal, the *project* of this new (modern) perspective.

As Enlightenment philosophers took over the process of *rationalization*, subtle changes occurred. Ernst Cassirer has noted that "reason" in the seventeenth century had to do with "those truths held in common by the human and divine mind." In the eighteenth century, however, reason became "the original intellectual force which guides the discovery and determination of truth" (1979:13). Instead of a commonality between God and humankind, reason became a tool to discover and determine truth. Ultimate truth was not provided by divine revelation, it was discovered by human rational. This subtle but significant change impacted the development of Western culture in many ways—which will become apparent as we proceed.

Religion, of course, rooted in divine revelation, did not escape the scrutiny of human rational. The cruelty and devastation of the religiously motivated Thirty Years War (1618-1648), which was rooted in political and economic disputes between Catholics and Protestants, did not help matters any. A number of critical thinkers began to see organized religion as a great evil in society (Byrne 1996:28). An institution as powerful as the church, even though it was by then split into opposing Catholic and Protestant factions, had to be controlled and, if possible, minimized. This was so because, as far as the critical philosophers believed, much of the theology of the church was rooted in tradition and superstition rather than scientific inquiry. To be functional in a rational society, religion had to be rational. The mystical, supernatural aspects of Christianity had to be eliminated. The Bible had to be *demystified.*

For many during that time, deism (the belief that God created the universe but is no longer active in the ongoing affairs of the world) became a way to believe in God without all the irrational trappings of the supernatural (Jacob 2001:16). Eventually, for many Enlightenment thinkers, God himself became unnecessary and unwanted. The Christian humanism of the Renaissance gave way to the *secular humanism* of the Enlightenment. For some, religion became not only unnecessary, it became an enemy, a target of ridicule and resentment. Modern atheism became a by-product of secular humanism (Byrne 1996:124-149).

It is important to note that the views of a few philosophers did not necessarily reflect the thinking of the average person of that day. Enlightenment thinkers did have an impact on Western culture. But the agenda of the most aggressive Enlightenment proponents, such as Voltaire—whose apparent goal was to rid society of organized religion—was never achieved.

Looking at a few Enlightenment philosophers individually may shed some light on some of the philosophical developments that were crucial in the shaping of Western culture.

John Locke

Locke (1632-1704) was a Christian philosopher who is credited with establishing the philosophical school referred to as *empiricism.* Empiricism affirms that the basis of all knowledge is experience; that true knowledge cannot be arrived at through a process of rational argumentation rooted in *a priori* assumptions—*a priori* meaning prior to or independent of experience. In Locke's view, individuals were born without innate knowledge, as if they were a blank sheet of paper (the opposite of Descartes' view[7]). Knowledge, then, that can actually be claimed as "knowledge," was the result of experience. He also believed that individuals were born good, independent, and equal, views which demonstrate the relationship between his philosophy and his theology.

Locke's empirical approach made him anti-rationalistic (in the strict philosophical sense of being opposed to Descartes' rationalistic approach). Locke, however, was still very much an advocate of the use of reason in establishing knowledge rather than merely accepting or believing something without using a logical process to establish it as true.

Locke's views as a political philosopher may have been that which secured his place in history. His concern was to "create a political philosophy based on laws of nature which reason and experience suggests will provide the best practical policy for the governing human communities" (Oliver 1999:83). Locke believed that human beings had a natural right to self-government. He argued that people have a natural tendency to form agreements with each other (societal standards or moral laws) to assure their survival and security. While there needs to be government to protect and enforce those agreements, governments that fail to recognize human need to determine the agreements are working against natural inclinations and are regressive. For example, governments that enact laws of taxation without the consent of the people are overstepping their authority, for people have the right to self-government. Locke also suggested that if a government disregarded a people's right to self-governance, those people had a right to rebel—an idea that became a reality in the American Revolution.

---

[7] Kenny insists that in reality Descartes and Locke were not that far apart (1998:208-210).

To ensure the proper relationship between government and people, Locke suggested that a governing agreement be drawn up—a constitution outlining duties, obligations, rights, and limitations. He also suggested that the best form of government structure would include a separation of powers into three branches: legislative, executive, and judicial.

Locke's empiricism became the foundation for modern social sciences, and his political views and suggestions were utilized in the sociopolitical structuring of America. He is one of the most influential figures of the Enlightenment. While his belief in the basic goodness of humanity may have run counter to Augustinian theology, his reasoned empiricism is not anti-Christian in any way.

David Hume

Another key figure in Enlightenment philosophy was David Hume, the Scottish *skeptic*[8] (1711-1776). Hume was an empiricist, believing that all knowledge that could actually qualify as knowledge came through experience. However, he also realized the subjective and therefore self-limiting nature of interpreting (understanding, categorizing, utilizing) one's experiences. Therefore, he was *skeptical* that one's experience could provide a true and reliable sense of reality (Brown 1990:235-258). Specifically, Hume felt that human perception involved two features: impressions and ideas. Impressions were formed as a result, or grew out of, experience. An individual experiences something and that experience results in an impression being formed in his mind. From an impression the individual formulates an idea. Obviously the ideas, which grow out of impressions, which

---

[8] Grayling suggests that the Scottish philosopher Thomas Reid, who painted Hume as a radical skeptic, may be responsible for a view of Hume's work that is not entirely correct (1995:526-527).

grow out of experiences, are subjective and cannot be definitive in any sense of the word.

Hume's skepticism in the value of reason (either rationalistic or empirical) as a means of discovering ultimate objective truth became foundational in the approach of counter-Enlightenment Romantic philosophers. And it is a Hume-like skepticism in reason as an avenue for achieving ultimate objective truth that has been expressed by contemporary postmodern philosophers in what they refer to as the Enlightenment project.

Many would suggest that Hume's skepticism became an important negative factor in Enlightenment thinking because it lent itself to the development of atheistic conclusions. Perhaps the value of his work lies in exposing the limitations of human reason as an ultimate, objective method of discovering ultimate truth. For Hume, human reason is subjective and cannot, therefore, be relied upon for objective conclusions. Hume's point regarding the nature of human rational has been an important feature in the development of Western culture, especially of late.

Immanuel Kant

Kant (1724-1804) was a German philosopher who is considered one of the most influential thinkers of modern times. He was also a pious Christian (Scruton 1995:470). He had been schooled in the rationalistic school of philosophy (Brown 1990:312), but when he read Hume's work he began to consider the limitations of a rationalistic approach. However, he also realized the limitation of a purely empiricist approach. To a degree, his work was an attempt to develop a critical approach to philosophy that synthesized both the rationalist and the empiricist systems. However, Brown points out that Kant's theory of knowledge "boils down to the claim that. . ."

There is no description of the world that can free itself from experience. Although the world we know is not our creation, nor merely a synopsis of our perspective, it cannot be known except from the point of view which is ours. All attempts to break through the limits imposed by experience end in self-contradiction, and knowledge can never be ours (1990:316).

Though Kant referred to himself as a "pure rationalist" (Hare 2000:365-366), he sounds more like an empiricist. *You cannot know that which you cannot experience.* Yet a note of Hume-like skepticism also permeates his conclusion, for he notes that one "knows" or draws conclusions from experience only from his own personal point of view. Thus, that which one knows is subjective rather than objective.

Kant believed that humankind's moral responsibilities sprang from the fact that human beings were rational beings. Morality could not be dictated by an external authority, but came from within the rational creature. Unfortunately, Kant's position results in a moral relativity that opens the door for just about any kind of moral behavior that humans can justify as rational. Kant himself would not have suggested such, but his suggestion that morality comes from within the person eventually ends in subjectivity morality. The consequences of this have had a significant negative impact (from a Christian point of view) on Western culture.

Voltaire

Voltaire (1694-1778) was a French proponent of the Enlightenment. Whether or not to refer to him as a philosopher is open to discussion. Some philosopher-historians will include him as an Enlightenment philosopher while others will not. Voltaire studied and wrote about philosophy and science, especially focusing on Lockean and Newtonian ideas. He did not, however, contribute to

Enlightenment philosophy himself. Perhaps, therefore, it is best to refer to him as an advocate or proponent of Enlightenment thinking.

Voltaire is best known for his militant attacks on institutionalized religion, that is, on the church. Cassirer notes that Voltaire made a careful distinction in his writings between faith and superstition, between religion and the institutionalized church, which he saw as advocating superstition and fanaticism, standing in the way of knowledge and progress (1979:134). Voltaire's disciples, however, did not make the same distinctions. Voltaire was a deist, acknowledging God's existence, but denying his active presence in the world. He attacked the system of religion presented in the Old Testament, considering it primitive and savage (Brown 1990:292). His goal was to wipe out that which he considered superstitious and fanatical—traits he considered to be integral parts of organized religion.

Though Voltaire made no original contribution to Enlightenment philosophy, he preached secular humanism very effectively. In addition to his Philosophical Dictionary, he wrote novels, poems, and plays that expressed the radical secular views (empiricist in perspective) he had accepted during a three year stay in England.

Philosophy and Religion during the Enlightenment

Alistair Mason points out that while in some respects the Enlightenment became a dangerous antagonist of Christianity, the movement itself had Christian roots. He also notes that historians have often overstated the impact of a few deist or atheist philosophers on what was largely Christian Europe (2000:200-201).

The Enlightenment gave birth to a few outspoken anti-Christian thinkers. Their voices were not without impact. However, the West in general did not abandon its Christian heritage or become unchristian in its perspective.

Western Europe and the American colonies continued to be rooted in the Christian tradition. The Scottish branch of the Enlightenment was led mostly by Scottish clergymen. In America, Enlightenment thinking fueled the fires of revolution through church leaders who exhibited no hesitancy in interpreting Christianity in light of Lockean political philosophy. Most Americans, as most Europeans of that time, remained Christian in their orientation.

Many Enlightenment thinkers were ready to abandon institutionalized religion, but not their belief in God. The answer to their dilemma was the Enlightenment "rational" religion called deism. Deism allowed its devotees to believe in God without having him present in their lives or in the world in any real way. Deists *believed in God*, but reason *was their god*. Ultimate truth and morality were determined by human rationality not divine revelation. Deism was the religion of many of the philosophers. A more traditional form of Christianity, however, remained alive and well during the Enlightenment.

While many philosophers had abandoned the church and put God on a shelf in heaven (out of the way), most common folks remained very religious. Three very significant religious movements that impacted Western culture are Pietism, Methodism, and the modern missionary movement.

Pietism

The Reformers had focused most of their attention on matters of doctrine and the moral abuses of the clergy and other church officials. Their preaching and teaching was perceived by many as overly formal, dry, and for some, dead orthodoxy that offered little to assist people in personal spiritual formation and a closer walk with God. The Christian community (especially German Lutherans) reacting to the spiritual dullness of the mid to late 1600s began a movement known as *pietism*. The main thrust of pietism, as advocated by Philipp Jakob Spener, known as the father as pietism, was personal spiritual growth. Christians met together in small groups to study the Bible and encourage one another. For pietists, the focus was not on formal institutionalized religion, though they certainly did attend public worship, but on the private reflection of a personal faith expressed daily in a holy life. Personal Bible reading combined with acts of Christian charity and service characterized the pietistic movement.

Pietism developed in advance of the Enlightenment. Some historians have wondered if the individuality and private nature of the pietistic movement may have influenced Enlightenment thinkers in their emphases on privatizing religion, that is, removing it from the public arena (Noll 1984:856). Kant, for instance, was brought up in a pietistic home. The depth of influence pietism had on Enlightenment thinkers remains unknown. However, while Enlightenment philosophers were stressing the importance of human rationale, far greater numbers of pietistic Christians were stressing the importance of daily Bible reading and personal holiness.

Methodism

A movement similar to German pietism was the English Wesleyan Methodism of the early 1700s. As the pietists had, John and Charles Wesley stressed the inward nature of Christianity. It was to be a religion of the heart manifesting itself in personal holiness. John Wesley's Anglican religion was not providing him with the inward assurance he witnessed in Moravian (pietist) believers. His longings remained unfulfilled until he heard a layman expounding on Paul's letter to the Romans. The man's remarks were based on Luther's commentary on Romans, in which he stressed the importance of depending not on

140

oneself, but on Christ alone for salvation. As Wesley listened to the simple gospel preached with evangelistic fervor, knowing that he was indeed trusting Christ for his salvation, his heart warmed within him. He knew he had found the solution to his spiritual dilemma—a simple message preached effectively that produced a faith in Christ and changed one's life.

The key to the success of both pietism and Methodism was small group meetings that stressed Bible reading and personal holiness. While Enlightenment philosophy impacted the thinking and behavior of many people, Christianity, especially as it was expressed through pietism and Methodism, impacted the thinking and behavior of even greater numbers. Enlightenment thinkers advocated human rationale as the ultimate source for discovering and determining truth and morality. At the same time, Christians were advocating God's message contained in the Scriptures as the ultimate source of spiritual truth and moral guidance. What had begun in the Renaissance as Christian humanism, advocating the dignity and importance of humanity but allowing God to remain God, had, in the Enlightenment, degenerated into secular humanism, giving God lip-service but effectively replacing him with human rationality. Fortunately, Christianity was present to stem the tide of absolute rationalistic relativity. Pietism and Methodism were two movements that stemmed the tide of secular humanism during the "enlightenment" of Western culture.

The Modern Missionary Movement

While some Enlightenment proponents, such as Voltaire, were attacking the church, advocating the removal of religion from the public sphere, Christians were coming alive with missionary zeal because of the discovery of far away lands and primitive peoples (as they considered them) who did not know God. J. Herbert Kane suggests that the modern missionary movement was a direct result of German pietism (1982:76-77). The personal piety stressed by the pietists resulted in evangelistic zeal which manifested itself in missionary activity. The 1700s and 1800s witnessed a revival of missionary activity reminiscent of the first century.

William Carey's mission to India (1792) is typically noted as the beginning of the modern era of Christian missionary activity. However, "modern" mission outreach to foreign lands began during the Renaissance with the global exploration characteristic of that age. During the early years of the Enlightenment as well, Christian missionaries traveled all over the world.

Kane (1982:79) notes the locations and numbers of Moravian missions during the mid-1700s:

1732, St. Thomas in the Virgin Islands,
1733, Greenland,
1734, St Croix,
1735, Surinam,
1737, the Gold Coast and South Africa,
1740, North America,
1754, Jamaica,
1756, Antigua,
And between 1732 and 1760, 226 Moravian missionaries entered ten foreign countries.

The Moravians, of course, were only one Christian group. Others were also sending missionaries during that time.

It was during the pre-Enlightenment and Enlightenment that philosophy separated itself from theology and ran on a separate track, beyond the reach and control of the church. There were disagreements between theologians and philosophers, but many of the philosophers themselves were Christians, and belief in and honor for God remained part of their perspective.

With the elevation of human reason carried to its logical end, God became irrelevant for some Enlightenment thinkers. Christianity, however, continued to thrive, providing a balance against the damage that could have been done if absolute relativity had been promoted unchallenged in society. But it was challenged—by a developing evangelical form of Christianity that called for personal faith, holy living, and evangelistic zeal. Without this growing form of vocal, zealous Christianity, the secular humanism of Enlightenment philosophy may have impacted Western culture in more serious ways than it actually did.

Enlightenment Philosophy and Western Culture

Other than Christianity, Enlightenment philosophy has probably had more of an impact on Western culture than anything else. Christianity has had more of an impact because it has been around longer than Enlightenment philosophy and offers people something Enlightenment philosophy cannot: spiritual fulfillment, hope and heaven. Having said that, however, it is necessary to give credit where credit is due: Enlightenment philosophy has had a significant and lasting impact on Western culture.

Of course it is important to remember that Enlightenment philosophy would not have been possible had it not been for the Greeks and their naturalistic, individualistic, scientific way of thinking about the world. Enlightenment philosophy was the product of a long chain of thought and expression that occurred over 2000 years. So the forerunners of Enlightenment philosophy deserve some of the credit. Still, even if the tree's roots were nourished in the soil of ancient Greece, the fruit ripened in the fresh air and sunshine of the Enlightenment.

Enlightenment thinkers and doers knew they were following the path opened for them by Renaissance rebels who broke away from the intellectual tyranny that had stifled inquiry and analysis for so many centuries. As they followed the path, gaining momentum, they solidified new perspectives, new ways of thinking about the world, about scientific inquiry, about human beings and about what

143

humans could accomplish. What were the main components of Enlightenment thought that had such a profound impact on Western culture? They were:

1. The idea that the universe is orderly and rational and can be studied and understood. Of course the Greeks had known this long ago. But the idea was driven home and became part of the Western worldview during (or as a result of) the Enlightenment.

2. The idea that truth is accessible (because the universe is orderly and rational) and can be arrived at by means of empirical observation. Observations must be evaluated rationally, but observation is a valid means of studying and understanding our universe.

3. The idea that truth is understood in light of human experience. Humanity, the measure of all things, seeks out and identifies truth. An authority beyond human experience is not acceptable.

4. The idea that the universe, including biological life, can and should be viewed, studied, understood, and manipulated mechanistically. The universe is a machine. Study it like you would a machine.

5. The idea that religion should be a private concern and have no public presence.

6. The idea that the story of humanity is the story of progress, and that progress is the goal.

7. The idea that human life can be improved through education and rationality.

What underlying worldview assumptions would be necessary for ideas such as these to flourish? There are three.

First, for Enlightenment thinking to flourish, the universe would have to be thought of from a naturalistic point of view. That is, that it is based on physical laws where cause and effect can be analyzed and understood. The scientific terminology (naturalistic, physical laws, cause and effect) would not have to be present in one's assumptions, but the ideas they represent would have to be present.

When I was teaching in Nigeria I became aware of the difference between a naturalistic and a supernaturalistic point of view. People with a supernaturalistic perspective do not think in terms of physics and cause and effect in trying to understand why things happen. In fact, they do not ask, *why did this happen?* They think in terms of spirits or beings who cause things to happen. They ask, *who caused this to happen?*

A naturalistic worldview is rooted in a mechanistic perspective. The laws of physics are at work in the universe and things happen because a cause produces an effect, which becomes another cause producing another effect and so forth. Understanding the world is not a matter of what spirit or demon or god or annoyed ancestor did something. Understanding the world is a matter of investigation, analysis, experiment, observation, and rational explanation.

Because of the ancient Greeks and the subsequent rediscovery of classical philosophy in the Middle Ages, Renaissance thinkers developed a naturalistic worldview. Enlightenment thinkers inherited this naturalistic assumption about the world, perfected it and presented it in such a way that it became the accepted view or way of thinking about the cosmos.

Second, for Enlightenment thinking to flourish, people had to be thought of from an individualistic perspective rather than a group perspective. Again, lining up with the ancient Greeks, Renaissance and Enlightenment thinkers saw each human as an individual worthy of recognition, a person of value and dignity by virtue of his existence, an autonomous rational being capable of accomplishing good things and making progress. This individual had rights, had something to offer, and ought to be free to live in a way that he or she believed was right and good.

Again, my time in Nigeria helped me understand the difference between an individualistic and a group orientation in life. One day in class I asked a group of about 45 men what was the biggest difference between me as an American and themselves as Nigerians. Without having to discuss it, they knew the answer immediately. The biggest difference was that I conceived of myself first and foremost as an individual, while they conceived of themselves as part and parcel of their family and community. Africans (and most non-Western people) do not see themselves as individuals but as part of a group. Their identity, their very existence, is rooted in and flows from their family group. They do not think or act like individuals. Their connection to their group impacts every aspect of their lives. So, too, the Western individualistic orientation (the individualistic disconnect) impacts the way Western people live, especially in regards to relationships.

The individualistic orientation that can be traced all the way back to ancient Greece gave Western thinkers the freedom to rebel against accepted (group) thinking and ask and answer questions that would have otherwise been ignored.

An individualistic orientation in the worldview of Enlightenment thinkers allowed them to pursue a course of inquiry, investigation and theory that otherwise would have been impossible.

Third, for Enlightenment thinking to flourish the world and people had to be understood as rational in nature. The world had to be a rational world that could be studied and understood, and people had to be rational beings who could think critically and analytically so they could understand, cope with, and use (manipulate) the rational world.

Rational people in a rational world should not be held captive to fear, superstition, or emotionalism. The innate rational nature of people must be tapped and developed by

146

means of education. Rational people living in a rational world can make progress.

These three assumptions do not need to be linguistically formulated or expressed, but the basic assumptions about the nature of the world, a rational, law abiding, mechanistic world, and the nature of people, rational individuals, must be present in order for ideas such as those of the Enlightenment to flourish.

These three worldview assumptions became a standard part of the Western way of thinking about the world, about people, and about how life ought to be lived. They have impacted Western society deeply, and in combination with other deeply rooted worldview assumptions, especially those related to Judeo-Christian beliefs, have made the West what it is today and Americans who they are today.

Summary

The almost frenzied investigation, exploration and enterprise that characterized the height of Renaissance activity slowed and Europe settled into a more relaxed state for a while before the Enlightenment became fully energized. Between the two identifiable periods of growth and change three individuals stand out as important philosophers whose work fueled Enlightenment thinking: Bacon, Descartes, and Spinoza.

Of the many Enlightenment philosophers that could be noted, I selected Locke, Hume, Kant, and Voltaire. Their work is reflective of the diversity of thought that characterized the Enlightenment.

It was during the Enlightenment that philosophy and theology seem to have finally parted ways, and some philosophers preferred that organized, institutionalized religion be eliminated altogether. However, the roots of Christianity were buried deep in the intellectual and

147

emotional soil of the Europe and that ancient faith wasn't going to be eliminated. Movements sprang up, some before the Enlightenment, some during, that focused attention on inner faith and holy living, but those private expressions of faith were publicly displayed in participation in the institutionalized church.

A naturalistic, rationalistic, individualistic worldview was being formed in the West. But Judeo-Christian assumptions were already firmly entrenched in the Western mind and were not about to be replaced. Enlightenment assumptions were accepted and blended with Judeo-Christian assumptions to create a new perspective on the world and life.

Chapter 8

The Founding of America

The religious Reformation of Europe combined with the philosophical expressions of pre-Enlightenment and Enlightenment thinkers had a significant impact on the founding of America. Freedom of religion was a major concern in the establishment of American society (Eidsmoe 1987:11). So was the desire for a republican form of government, that is, a government in which elected officials carried out the collective will of the people. The dilemma was how to establish a government strong enough to accomplish its purpose (to protect, serve, and manage society) without trampling on the rights of those people.

Religion in the Early Days of the American Colonies

Many of the people who migrated to America in the 1600s and 1700s did so to escape religious persecution. The earliest Christian influence in America came from the Puritans and Quakers. They wanted to be free to worship God according to their consciences. Unfortunately, their beliefs and traditions were unacceptable in Europe (Hutson 1998:3). European Christians were still struggling with the difficulties that resulted from the Reformation. Catholics and Protestants from various segments of the Reformation believed that theirs was the one true expression of the ancient Christian faith. Religious wars and persecution, accusations and recriminations, made the whole religious scene in Europe an ugly mess. No wonder so many Enlightenment thinkers, who recognized the foolish arrogance of Christians for what it was, became disenchanted with institutionalized religion in those days.

The astonishing thing is that those who fled to America to escape religious persecution became as intolerant of other expressions of Christianity as the religious leaders in Europe had been of theirs. The goal of the Puritans was to establish a society that was governed by religious authority. Magistrates were to be "public ministers of God" (Hutson 1998:7). They wanted to create a unified society based on their view of Scripture and theology. Such a society, however, is by nature intolerant of the beliefs and practices of others. Fortunately, this inherent weakness was recognized and alternative societal structures were put into place. We have Enlightenment thinking to thank for that.

The Quakers are considered by some historians to be a more radical branch of the Puritan faith. In addition to sharing the Puritan goal of continued reformation, Quakers believed in spiritual illumination (direct guidance from the Holy Spirit that made most organized religions irrelevant) and advocated complete equality between the sexes (Hutson 1998:8-10). One of their leaders in Pennsylvania was William Penn. In 1682, he advocated "liberty to all peoples to worship God according to their faith and persuasion" (12). Penn believed that people with diverse religious views could live together peaceably. It was an idea that others also began to promote. Eventually, even Puritans, who had been opposed to religious toleration, came to see the importance of religious freedom and toleration.

Religion in the American colonies in the 1700s was a vast mosaic of feverish activity. Estimates are that in the years between 1700 and 1740, 75 to 80 percent of the American people attended church with some frequency (Hutson 1998:24). Puritans, Quakers, Anglicans, Presbyterians, Methodists, Baptists, Catholics, Lutherans, Dutch Reformed and others practiced their religious beliefs alongside one another in "relative" peace, though there were still unfriendly theological skirmishes. Even before religious freedom was written into governing documents, guaranteed as a right of the peoples of America, it was being practiced by the people on their own.

Enlightenment Thinking and the Founding of America

Enlightenment philosophers had a tremendous impact on the thinking of the men who played key roles in establishing the American Republic. Pre-Enlightenment thinkers such as Bacon, Descartes and Spinoza prepared the intellectual soil of Europe so Enlightenment philosophers such as Locke could plant the seeds of political evolution. Many American pastors were political activists who believed they ought to preach political reform as part of their religious message. Hutson notes that by the 1740s American churchmen were including portions of Locke's writings in their sermons, stressing the natural rights of all people.

Locke had put forth the idea of a "social contract." He believed that the *law of nature* included maintaining societal order and preserving individual rights. This required a social contract between people, agreeing to be governed so that order could be maintained and rights preserved. According to Locke, the contract or agreement was between the people (person to person) not between the people and the government. The government functioned within the framework of the social contract to preserve life, freedom, and ownership of property. If a government (regardless of its kind—monarchy or democracy) sought to gain absolute power, it put itself at odds with the people, creating a state of war. According to Locke, at that point the people had the right to overthrow that corrupt government and establish a new government (Brown 1990:221-222). This political philosophy became part of the religious message preached in many of America's pulpits during the mid to late 1700s. It was a foundational concept in the larger sociopolitical ideology that fueled the fires of revolution and was eventually included in the Constitution of the United States.

Philosophical and Religious Beliefs of America's Founding Fathers

Enlightenment philosophy impacted religious beliefs as much as it did political ideology. The secular humanism underlying a great deal of Enlightenment philosophy caused some people to abandon their belief in a God who was present and active in his world. They became atheists. Others found middle ground in deism, believing in God's existence, but denying his active presence in the world. Some of America's founding fathers were deists. However, John Eidsmoe argues that there were not as may deists among the founding fathers as some historians have suggested.

Eidsmoe, based on Bradford's research, argues that of the fifty-five delegates to the Constitutional Convention, only three of them, Hugh Williamson, James Wilson, and Benjamin Franklin, listed themselves as deists rather than as members of a specific church (1987:41-43). And even though Franklin listed himself as a deist, his own comments make it clear that he believed in a God who is involved in the affairs of humanity, a God who answers prayers. In a speech to the Constitutional Convention delivered on June 28, 1774, Franklin referred to God as our "powerful friend." He went on to say that, "the longer I live the more convincing proofs I see of this truth—that God governs in the affairs of men." Franklin then suggested that clergymen be invited to pray each morning during the convention to ask God's blessing on their deliberations (Hutson 1998:76). Franklin's comments are not consistent with his claims of being a deist. Eidsmoe concludes that deism never caught on in America as it did in Europe.

One key figure in early American history who is often linked with deism is Thomas Jefferson, perhaps the most influential figure in the founding and structuring of the American republic. In his earlier days (1770-1780) Jefferson seemed infatuated with secular moralism. Scholars, however, believe that around 1793 he read Joseph Priestley's book *An History of the Corruptions of Christianity*. Priestley's book, which set forth Jesus' moral teachings in a way that made sense to Jefferson, convinced Jefferson that he was, after all, a Christian.

In a letter Jefferson wrote in 1803 to a physician friend in Philadelphia, he said that he was a Christian in the only sense that Jesus wished anyone to be a Christian (Kramnick 1995:163), meaning that he believed in and adhered to the moral teachings of Jesus. Jefferson also attended church regularly throughout his term as President. He was also an avid biblical scholar, producing a forty-six page treatise on the authentic sayings of Jesus. He completed this work in 1804 while serving as President (Hutson 1998:83-93). As Jefferson's own faith grew he became more convinced of the value of faith in society and government. He went so far as to suggest that it was essential for the "promotion of public morality" that people believe in heaven and hell—not the exact words he used but clearly what he meant (84). Clearly, Thomas Jefferson espoused the basics of a Christian faith and attempted to reflect those beliefs in his behavior, including his regular church attendance throughout his presidency.

Generally speaking, nearly all of America's founding fathers were Christians. As noted earlier, all but three of the individuals who attended the Constitutional Convention in

1774 listed themselves as member of a Christian church. Of course merely listing themselves as members of a church does not mean that they were Christians in any meaningful sense of the word. However, when the congress met in September 1774 their first order of business was to select a Christian minister to open their sessions with a prayer. Then, one of the first decisions of the congress was to declare a national day of public humiliation, fasting, and prayer for forgiveness and blessings from God. Congress collectively adopted a covenant theology which adhered to the idea that America was party to a covenant (an agreement) with God in which he promised to punish sins and reward obedience on the national level, as he had with Israel in the Old Testament. For ten years, between June 1775 and August 1784, Congress preached this message to the people of America by means of an annual proclamation (Hutson 1998 51-53). The founders of America were men of Christian faith.

Religion and the American Government

The Articles of Confederation had not made provision for a federal government strong enough to govern well. Something more was needed. At the same time, however, it remained important that the federal government not be given too much power, power it could abuse in the trampling of individual rights. The framers of the Constitution were walking a sociopolitical tightrope. To get the Constitution passed, it had to appeal to as wide an audience as possible. It also needed to avoid duplication of matters that were under state control, such as matters of religion. Thus, the Constitution made no mention of religion. That did not mean, however, that God and religion had no place in the government of the new country. It meant simply that in the Constitution itself there would be no legislation regarding religion. However, as the leaders began

154

working on the Bill of Rights (which is a more detailed statement of governmental powers and individual rights) the First Amendment to the Constitution guaranteed that *"Congress shall make no law respecting an establishment of religion, or prohibiting the free exercise thereof."* America was to be a country where people were free to worship according to the dictates of their consciences. The government cannot control religion in any way. There is no established, recognized, official national religion and the government cannot interfere in any way with the free exercise of religion. This was the only way to guarantee religious freedom to all people, which was, after all, why the original immigrants had come to America in the first place—to enjoy religious freedom.

There has been a great deal of discussion in recent years as to whether or not America is a Christian nation. Gary DeMar suggests that America has always been considered a Christian nation because Christianity is the dominant religion of Americans by a wide margin, and because the founding fathers purposefully set out to establish a Christian nation that allowed freedom of religion for all people (2003:7-12). It is not that all Americans are Christians or that all American Christians live as they ought to live. Many people, including some who claim to be Christians, live lives that are very *un*christian. However, many of the guiding principles and values upon which this country was founded grew out of the Judeo-Christian tradition. The underlying moral code that provides the foundation of American society is Judeo-Christian. Many would argue, therefore, that America is a Christian nation. However, many would also argue, that America is not a Christian nation because there is no stated national religion. It cannot be denied, however, that Christianity played a major role in the development of American culture and continues to impact American society.

Philosophy, Religion and Revolution

It is important to note that Christianity is not a religion of political revolution. As domineering and oppressive as the Roman Empire was, Christians in the first century were taught to submit, to obey laws, to honor government officials, to pay taxes—in short, to be good citizens. There is not a single element in Christianity that would lead believers to engage in political revolution.

How then did preachers in colonial America justify their politically oriented sermons, their political activism? They had accepted Lockean political philosophy and were determined to voice their opinions and exercise their rights. Believing their cause to be just, they sought to enlist God's support in their campaign against British tyranny. They also sought to rally additional support by enlisting the aid of their congregations. If everyone believed that it was God's will to establish a new country, based on the freedoms and individual rights the Creator had given them, they would be more determined to stand their ground. (Notice the worldview assumptions about the nature of human beings inherent in their thinking.)

In reality, of course, there is a great deal of difference between Lockean political philosophy and the theology of Jesus and Paul. Neither Jesus nor Paul was a revolutionary. Neither advocated political activism. They advocated holy living and submission to government authority. It is not that Christian faith and political activism are mutually exclusive. They are not. But there is nothing in Christianity that requires political activism, nothing that compels one to engage in revolution against an established government, regardless of how corrupt it may be. If a believer engages in political revolution it is because of his or her political philosophy not because of Christianity. However, the Christian faith is lived out in the context of a believer's

156

sociopolitical circumstances, and those circumstances are going to impact the way Christianity is understood and lived.

In the American colonies, resentment toward the tyranny of Great Britain and the desire to be free combined with their Christian and Enlightenment view of humanity (created in God's image and in possession of certain inalienable rights) to generate a spirit of defiance toward anyone who would trample those rights. Add to that some Lockean philosophy that granted them the right to rebel and establish a new government, and you have a revolution. The foundation for the American Revolution was far more Lockean than Christian.

Christianity and Early American Culture

Having said that, however, it is important to note that it was the desire for religious freedom that brought the first settlers to America—and the religion in question was Christianity. Those immigrants did not arrive in the new land empty handed. They brought their culture with them. By 1650, the Dutch, English, French, Spanish, and Swedish had established settlements in the new world. The culture of early America was the culture these immigrants brought with them. Some would have been happy to duplicate their home culture in their new American context. Others preferred to make some adjustments, especially in the areas of government and religion. Many of the cultural practices of the old world were incorporated into the new emerging American society. But most were modified and adapted to the specific needs of a new life context, a rapidly evolving and somewhat experimental context. A specific and unique American culture was developing and evolving.

Since many of the people who came to America were seeking religious freedom, their lives were deeply rooted in spiritual concerns. Their faith, which impacted their daily lives in many ways, was reflected most clearly in their home

157

and family life. The husband was the head and spiritual leader of the family (though often a spiritually mature wife provided the encouragement and impetus her husband needed to fulfill his societal role). Daily Bible reading and prayers were common practices. Many children learned to read by reading the Bible. Moral standards were high and ungodly behavior was not tolerated, especially in regions dominated by Puritan influence. Sunday was a day of worship and families went to church together unless they were too far into the wilderness for there to be a church nearby. In those cases families would worship in their homes.

The importance of Christianity in the developing American culture becomes clear when one considers the growth of churches (in number and in size) in the early days of American history:

> In 1660 the largest denomination was the Congregationalists, with 75 churches, followed by the Anglicans, with 41. Then, further behind, came the Dutch Reformed, with 13 churches, Roman Catholics, with 12; Presbyterians, with 5; Lutherans and Baptists, with 4 each; and Jews, with 1 synagogue.
>
> By 1780 [120 years later], there had been startling changes both quantitatively and qualitatively. The largest denomination was still the Congregationalists, with 749 churches. But there were three denominations vying for second place: the Presbyterians, who had 495 churches; the Baptists, with 457; and the Anglicans/Episcopalians, with 406. The German Reformed church, with 201 churches, and the Dutch Reformed church, with 127 churches, combined for a total of 328 Reformed churches. The Catholics and Jews had also grown, but at a slower pace: The Catholics had 56 churches, the Jews 6 synagogues (Kosmin and Lachman 1993:28).

As noted earlier, in the years between 1700 and 1740, 75 to 80 percent of the American people attended church with some frequency (Hutson 1998:24). Given these statistical realities, it would be hard to overestimate the role of Christianity in the emerging American culture. America was indeed, as the phrase in the Pledge of Allegiance suggests, "one nation *under God.*"

Understanding Americans

Why all this focus on Religion? What does it have to do with understanding contemporary American culture? The fruit of the tree is impacted by the roots and the soil. The history of a people—who they have been—tells us a great deal about who they are. The emergence of modern Western culture out of the dark centuries that followed the fall of Rome involved the impact of two major forces: Christianity and the rediscovery of Greek classical philosophy. Tracing how those two forces collided and blended to shape Western society is crucial to understanding why Americans (especially Anglos) are the way they are. Understanding the forces that shaped America, theologically and philosophically is crucial to understanding why Americans are they way they are.

Many secular historians attempt to minimize the role of Christianity in the shaping of America. To do so is something like attempting to minimize the role of flour in baking a cake. It is not possible to understand the shaping of America without understanding the role of Christianity in the shaping process.

So to understand Americans it is essential to understand the forces that shaped their worldview. The two most significant forces were Greek philosophy (which gave birth to pre-Enlightenment and Enlightenment philosophy), and Christianity. The blending of these two forces is what has made the West the West.

In seeking to understand Americans it is also helpful to keep in mind the character of the people that settled America. The people who left Europe with their Judeo-Christian, Greek, Enlightenment Western worldview were

159

(generally speaking): stubborn, strong, committed, brave, determined, deeply religious, inventive, hard working, visionary, sacrificial, defiant people who were going to build a better life for themselves and their families or die trying. And many of them did die. But still, more like them came. Give a strong, defiant, capable people a Judeo-Christian, Greek, Enlightenment worldview and America is what you get.

Summary

Many of the people who colonized America came here to escape religious persecution. They wanted to live in a place where they were free to worship and live as their faith dictated. The founding of America is rooted in religious freedom. The religion in question was Christianity. The moral and ethical foundation upon which America was built is Judeo-Christian. But it was a decidedly Western form of the Judeo-Christian tradition. Greek philosophy, rediscovered in Europe during the late Middle Ages, had become a part of the Western worldview. The collision and subsequent blending of philosophy and theology followed by the separation of the two disciplines created a unique Western way of thinking about the world and life in the world. The moral foundation of the Judeo-Christian tradition and the naturalistic, rationalistic, humanistic foundation of Enlightenment philosophy combined to create a worldview that allowed for freedom of thought, expression, exploration and experimentation socially, politically, economically, and technologically within a basic framework of morality and justice. The West was not a perfect place, but it was a unique place. The conglomeration of European peoples that comprised Western culture at that time were not a perfect people. But because of their character and their worldview they were a unique people.

160

Chapter 9

Contemporary American Culture

Christianity and Enlightenment philosophy collided and combined to create a unique Western worldview that allowed the West to become what it is. But those forces shaped America over 200 years ago. Is there a more recent development that must be factored in if we are to understand why Americans are the way they are? Yes. It is the development of Postmodernity.

The Development of Postmodernity

Many people during the early Middle Ages were illiterate. It was a time of superstition and fear. But with the rediscovery of classical philosophy a few scholars of the late Middle Ages began to think differently, blending philosophy and theology with exciting results. They began to realize that it was possible to believe in God but think about the world, as the Greeks had, from a naturalistic, humanistic, rationalistic perspective.

The Birth of Modernity

During the Renaissance, thinkers such as Leonardo da Vinci, Nicolas Copernicus, Francis Bacon, René Descartes, Isaac Newton, and later men like Thomas Hobbs and John Locke set the stage for the development of the modern scientific perspective. Human reason was elevated to center stage. Descartes, for instance, "defined human nature as a thinking substance and the human person as an autonomous rational subject," (Grenz 1996:3). Francis Bacon suggested that rational knowledge (that is, scientific knowledge) "should be used as a tool for mastering the natural world," giving humans "the ability to control and predict," (Van Gelder 1996:117). Newton pictured the physical universe as a machine regulated by laws of physics. It could be studied, understood, and manipulated by humans for human benefit.

The information humans needed to control their world was available. Thorough, specific, and precise knowledge could be acquired and used. Facts you could "know" through scientific processes became paramount. Spiritual concerns, which were not subject to rational investigation and scientific verification, were considered unimportant, assigned to the realm of private speculation. From a scientific perspective, however, the universe, like a gigantic machine, could be understood and manipulated through examination and experimentation. Science and human reason became the dominant focus of many of the scholars of Western culture, pushing God and spiritual things into the shadowy realm of the unverifiable and therefore the unimportant.

Ultimately, the combination of Descartes' philosophy and Newton's science resulted in a "modern" way of thinking about human beings and the physical world which, as Grenz suggests, amounted to *the rational individual encountering the mechanistic world.* As this *modern* approach to life evolved, its goal was to bring "rational management to life in order to improve human existence through technology" (1996:3). In other words, human beings, exercising the power of their rationale, utilizing sound scientific processes and procedures, could unlock the secrets of the universe, finding answers to life's questions, and solutions to life's problems. As far as Enlightenment thinkers were concerned, "the best hope for the betterment of humankind is the progress which occurs as societies throw off the vestiges of a past dominated by superstition and myth," (Stangroom and Garvey 2005:73). Through scientific investigation and experimentation, humans could unlock the secrets of the universe. They could know the knowable. This expectation of knowledge and progress though scientific processes was a "modern" way of thinking. It became known as *modernity*. Simply put, the goal of modernity was human progress. Progress became the *modern project*.

Human reason and scientific process were the hallmarks of *modernity*. Rationale and process, logic and syllogism, individuality and determination were the theoretical engines that drove the modern Western machine of technological progress. The grand scheme of the modern project was summed up in the phrase, *"Every day in every way we're getting better and better."*

The foundational ideas of modernity—the autonomous, rational being encountering the mechanistic world—laid the ground work for the development of a number of subordinate ideas that are important features of the larger Western worldview. As noted previously, individualism is one of the most basic concepts of the Western worldview. Descartes' *autonomous rational being* is first and foremost an individual. He is not part and parcel of a group. He does not give up his individuality to the will of the group. As my Nigerian students observed, this individual orientation is one of the key features of a Western perspective on life.

Another key feature of the typical modernistic Western worldview is a naturalistic (as opposed to a supernaturalistic) orientation. For modernistic people, the universe is impersonal and mechanistic, operating according to physical laws. It is dependable and predictable. The laws of physics can be studied and manipulated. We can dive to the depths of the ocean, travel to the moon and beyond; we can cure disease and manipulate human development and behavior at the genetic level. When we are sick, there is a naturalistic, scientific reason and response. We can go to the scientist (doctor) who can discover the reason for the sickness and prescribe a scientific response to the problem.

Since the world works according to predictable rules, we can predict certain eventualities. Just as the laws of physics allow us to predict certain physical phenomena, so the laws of economics allow us to predict certain economic phenomena. Capitalism, as an economic system, is a product of modernity, an outgrowth of the scientific *cause and effect* way of thinking applied specifically to economics.

A great deal of our Western worldview has been shaped by the modernistic (naturalistic, rationalistic) way of thinking about the world and human beings. For instance, we think and reason in a linear fashion, we reason things out syllogistically; we analyze things from a cause and effect perspective. We draw lines of demarcation between the physical and the spiritual, between the rational and the emotional—because we are first and foremost rationalistic and naturalistic in our perspective. For centuries, the Western educational system has been rooted in modernity— though this is in the process of changing. What we teach our children, and the way we teach them, has grown out of our naturalistic, rationalistic perspective on life.

I could go on, but this is sufficient to make the point: the typical Western worldview has been shaped considerably (not solely, but considerably) by modernity. Even Christianity did not escape its influence. Western Christianity is a modernistic version of the ancient faith.

Challenging Modernity's Assumptions

The foundation for modernity had been laid during the Renaissance and the building built during the Enlightenment. In the late 1800s, Fredrick Nietzsche laid another foundation which would lead philosophers to question the premises of the modern perspective. Could science really provide all the answers? Could human beings, using scientific methodologies, really solve all of life's problems? The answer for a number of philosophers was, no. Through the early 1900s a wave of disenchantment with the modernistic perspective grew and by the mid 1900s many philosophers had abandoned modernistic premises.

To a number of philosophers, the idea that humans could know precisely, accurately, and thoroughly, gaining insight into reality that was beyond the subjectivity of personal and cultural parameters, was absurd. They insisted that all perception was culturally and personally impacted, and that there was no such thing as objectivity, scientific or otherwise. What did they mean?

They recognized that our sense perceptions of reality are impacted by our personal and cultural context, by our assumptions, our expectations, and our experiences—as Bacon had pointed out. Sense perception, far from being objective, is highly subjective. For example, gender impacts sense perception. Husbands who have gone clothes shopping with their wives soon realize that while they see basic colors (red, blue, green, yellow, brown, tan, gray, black) their wives see dozens of shades in between each of the shades their husbands recognize. Why is this? There are two reasons. First, women's brains are wired differently. They notice more color and texture, while men's brains are wired so they are more visually sensitive to movement. Second, because women's brains and eyes are more interested in and see more color variation, they have more categories and names for colors than most men.

Some would question the validity of such arguments, noting that men see as many colors as women. Perhaps they do. But few men consider the slight differences important enough to designate them as separate colors. For most men, for example, light green, green, or dark green is precise enough. For most women those three designations would not be precise enough. The latest brain research indicates that gender impacts perception and the articulation of perception (Moir and Jessel 1991).

Culture also impacts what one sees. When I lived in Nigeria it became apparent to me that Nigerians do not see lines and angles the same way Americans or Europeans do. Because of our Western interest in and focus on mathematics, we are trained to think and see in geometric terms. Because of our scientific orientation, details also matter to us. When building a building it matters to us that lines are straight. Right angles matter! And when something is out of alignment we can see it. Most Nigerian carpenters who framed doors and windows could not "see" when an angle was off. They would have to measure to see it. The Americans there could simply look at it and see that it was not straight. Why? Because angles and lines and details are important to us. We think in those terms so we see in those terms. Nigerians don't. So they do not "see" that a door frame is not square. Perception is impacted by cultural factors as well as personal considerations, such as background, education gender, age, experience, and so forth. Let us refer to these various factors as *perspective*. One's perspective impacts one's perception.

This is true for all people in all places. A REALITY beyond ourselves exists. We are part of the cosmos. But REALITY is culturally and personally perceived. That means there is REALITY (the really real) and there is my perception of it, my reality, which is impacted by a number of things (Hiebert 1999; Kraft 1996:14-19).

Given this insight, philosophers were quick to point out that an objective view of REALITY was not possible. Therefore, actual, precise knowledge of the universe is not possible. That which modernists said could be achieved could not be achieved. Absolute knowledge could not be achieved because it did not exist. Absolutes of any kind do not exist, some of them insisted. Everything is relative—absolutely relative.

Postmodernity

The rejection, by philosophers, of the basic tenants of modernism has led to what is now referred to as *post*modernism. It is called *post*modernism because it is a perspective that comes after modernism. It is not so much a new perspective as it is a denial of significant aspects of the modernistic perspective.

Postmodernism denies the supremacy of rationalism. From a postmodern perspective, experiences and emotions are just as important as reason. Postmodernism does not seek to dichotomize life, separating the material from the spiritual or the rational from the emotional. Postmodernism approaches life from a more holistic perspective, realizing that many of life's most important questions or considerations lie beyond the realm of scientific investigation. Metaphysics is more important than physics for most postmodernists. Because of postmodernism's focus on holism, some postmodernists are more interested in community than in individualism.

167

Postmodernism's Impact on American Culture

The postmodern philosophers who challenged the assumptions of modernism and suggested alternative philosophical paradigms were/are dealing in philosophy, which, for a lot of people does not often seem to have a lot to do with everyday life. Philosophers propose and argue concepts using philosophic jargon that the average person does not understand. Initially, what they proposed regarding modernity had little effect on society.

However, what they proposed did get discussed in college classrooms and other contexts where educated people shared ideas. As postmodern ideas were shared, some of them caught on. As young people who were exposed to postmodern ideas in college went to live and work in the real world, they took their newly acquired postmodern ideas with them and gradually postmodernism found its way into American society. Movies, books, songs, magazines, commercials and all sorts of other media were used to disseminate postmodern thinking. Eventually, the hardcore philosophical postmodernism of an elite group of academics trickled down into society to become popular cultural postmodernism.

The trickling down of postmodern ideas resulted in some mutation. Popular postmodernism is not as radical and hard-edged as some of the philosophical versions, but it is similar enough to go by the same name. How has postmodernism effected American culture?

First, it must be noted that even though postmodernism has rejected many of the basic tenants of modernism, postmodern people still have a basic Western worldview. Postmodern people do not place as much confidence in the rationalistic process as modernists do, but neither have they abandoned rationalism altogether.

Some postmodernists are not as individualistic as many modernists, but neither are they as group oriented as

168

Africans. Compared to Africans, postmodernists are still highly individualistic. Even though postmodernists approach life more holistically than modernists, postmodernists are still basically naturalistic (as opposed to supernaturalistic) in their perspective. They may be more interested in spiritual things than the previous generations of modernists were, but when compared to supernaturalistic people (Africans, for example) postmodernists are quite naturalistic.

American postmodernists (for the most part) are still capitalists. They are still time oriented rather than event oriented. Generally speaking, their space orientation has not changed. Their methods of categorization have remained unchanged. Some aspects of their thinking may have changed, but for the most part, postmodern people have the same (or at least many of the same) deep-level assumptions about life that modernistic Western people have. They still operate out of a typical Western worldview.

Having noted that, however, it is also important to highlight some of the differences in thinking exhibited by a generation of Americans impacted by postmodernism.

1. Few moral absolutes. A crucial difference in the thinking of individuals who have been impacted by postmodernism is their lack of concern for moral absolutes. For them, right and wrong are relative. Most postmodern Americans will draw the line at some of the bigger human abuses: child molestation, murder, rape. But for the "lesser evils" whether a thing is right or wrong depends on the circumstances.

This lack of concern for moral absolutes has manifested itself in a number of ways. Business ethics seem to have suffered a great deal in the postmodern social context. The corporate financial fraud and subsequent collapse of several major American companies can be traced to a kind of amorality that manifests itself in unprecedented levels of greed and lying, fraud and stealing, that in previous generations were not seen in American business—at least not at the present (or recent) levels.

169

Another area where the postmodern morality is evident is in matters related to sex. Just about any thing goes with sex in contemporary American society unless it involves children or animals. The whole idea of a God who has moral standards that he expects people to live by is not popular with many younger Americans.

2. *A dislike for outside authority.* Since, for postmodern people, everything (generally speaking) is relative, what is right or wrong is, for the most part, up to the individuals involved. So the individual's thinking regarding an issue under consideration matters more than anyone else's, including God's.

3. *Pluralistic tolerance.* Postmodern people believe that since there are few absolutes of any kind and little, if any, outside authority to which they answer, whatever people believe about just about anything is acceptable—as long as it doesn't hurt anyone. Postmodern people accept everyone: atheists, agnostics, Muslims, Buddhists, Hindus, even Christians (as long as the Christians don't express the idea that Christianity is the only true faith that God will accept). Among postmodern people, the only belief that isn't acceptable is the one that says not all beliefs are acceptable.

4. *A reader-response hermeneutic.* Some postmodern people believe that when you read something, it means whatever you decide it means. What the author who wrote it may have intended for it to mean is irrelevant. This lax approach to interpretation coincides with their general relativistic tendencies.

These four ideas can be found among many people (to varying degrees) who have been impacted by postmodernity. The impact of this philosophy on American culture has been significant, for a philosophy that espouses such a loose sense of morality espouses a social system that cannot survive. And to a degree, many Americans have adopted a decidedly postmodern perspective on life.

This is not to suggest that postmodernity has no redeeming virtues. It does. Postmodernity has refocused attention on the fact that human being are not merely rational machines, but emotional beings who feel as well as think, and that our emotions are a vital part of who we are. Postmodernity has refocused attention on the importance of spiritual things. If the rational-natural is not all-important, then the emotional-spiritual must be important as well. Postmodernism has made it acceptable to be intellectual and also be interested in spiritual matters.

Postmodernism has rightly pointed out the holistic nature of life and that rather than think of humans as machines, thinking of humans as complex organisms is preferable. Postmodernism has reminded scientists that their interpretation is not as objective as they had presumed, and has given a measure of validity and respectability to worldviews other than the Western naturalistic, rationalistic, individualistic worldview. By advocating pluralism, postmodernism has nudged Western people into a less ethnocentric perspective regarding other cultural systems.

The thing that makes a discussion like this difficult is that postmodernism is hard to define, and no two postmodern people are going to be alike. There is a great deal of variation between postmodernists on many things—as one would expect in a system where everything is relative. Like most philosophical systems, postmodernism has some negative features and some positive features. As a philosophical system that has trickled down into popular culture, it has impacted American society in significant ways. Contemporary Americans still hold to a basic Western worldview, but with a postmodern twist. In postmodern Western society there is an inclination away from authority and moral absolutes, toward relativity and pluralism. But even postmodern Americans are still individualistic, naturalistic, rationalistic Western people.

Some social observers have suggested that the influence of postmodernism and the subsequent pluralistic atmosphere that comes with it have thrust America into a *postchristian* era. Christians make up a lower percentage of the total population than they used to and there has been an increase in antichristian sentiment and rhetoric. However, according to the Barna Group (2006), in 2005 47 percent of Americans still attended a Christian worship service each week. That means that nearly half of the U.S. population is still made up of Christians who are committed enough to their faith to attend church regularly. Perhaps suggesting that America is postchristian is a bit premature. However, the impact of postmodernism on American society is undeniable.

Are the Postmodernists Right

Are the postmodernists right in their critique of modernism? Yes, and no. It depends on what aspect of modernity is under consideration and what corrective measures or alternative perspectives are suggested.

Postmodernists are right in saying that there is a great deal of relativity in just about every aspect of life. Given that truth, a definitive answer on the merits of two different philosophical systems (modernity or Postmodernity) is difficult to arrive at. Some aspects of modernism needed to be challenged. The hyper naturalistic, rationalistic focus of modernity created an imbalance. Modernity has exhibited little interest in the spiritual or emotive/intuitive aspects of life. Postmodernists have addressed that imbalance. But some aspects of postmodernism go too far, creating an imbalance in the other direction that is just as unhealthy.

Postmodernists are right in noting that perception is impacted by perspective. REALITY is culturally and personally perceived. But to begin with that realization and conclude that there are no moral absolutes, that everything is completely relativity, is simply unwarranted.

Postmodernists have encouraged respect and tolerance of beliefs other than one's own. That is good. But for postmodernists, that respect and tolerance grows of out the idea that ultimate truth is unknowable, that there are no absolutes, that everything is relative, and, therefore, that all beliefs are equally valid. This is pluralism. On a practical level, tolerance for other belief systems and respect for those who hold them is good. But ultimately, pluralism without a foundation of moral absolutes leads to the moral decay and decline of society.

In considering the relative merits of each philosophical system it is important to acknowledge that even with all the shortcomings of modernity, it is the naturalistic, rationalistic, scientific, individualistic, humanistic focus of modernity that has made America the strongest nation on earth. Thanks to modernity we are an educated, technologically advanced, wealthy, powerful nation that enjoys the enumerable benefits of science and medicine. Modernity, not postmodernity, gets the credit for those advances. In fact, some of the progress modernity promised has been realized.

Summary

With the rediscovery of classical philosophy the intellectually bleak early Middle Ages came alive. Scholars began to think, to question, to reposition themselves. New perspectives allowed for new perceptions. The late Middle Ages blossomed into the Renaissance and the kind of thinking that had characterized the ancient Greeks energized Europe. The freedom to think gave birth to new ideas. Renaissance became Enlightenment and modernism was born. Enlightenment promised further illumination. Science promised progress.

Everything was subject to scientific investigation and critique. That which could not bear the close scrutiny of scientific methodology was discarded. Science, as the tool of rational inquiry into the naturalistic, mechanistic world became god. Science was the method, knowledge the aim, progress the goal. The secrets of the universe lay before humankind. We had but to discover and use them to our benefit. Hunger and sickness and war and suffering could be eliminated. What God had been unable or unwilling to accomplish (if indeed there was a God) humankind could do!

Eventually, however, it became painfully clear that humankind was not going to be able to accomplish all that much, even with its new scientific tools. As the Renaissance had come to an end, so did the Enlightenment. Not long after, the 20th century began the promise of a better world though enlightenment was lost in World War I. Then came the depression. Then came World War II; then the Korean War; then Communism and the Cold War; then Vietnam. And along the way, during and after, right up to the present there has been famine, disaster, genocide (in half a dozen cultural contexts, not just one), epidemic, pandemic, brutality, injustice, and oppression. Modernity has not kept its promise.

So postmodernists pop up pointing out the weaknesses of modernity. And rightfully so, for there are many weaknesses in modernity, arrogance being one of them. Instead of seeking ultimate truth, postmodernists point out, we should realize that perhaps there is no ultimate truth, or if there is, it is beyond our grasp. Therefore the only reasonable course is one of relativity and pluralism. There is enough truth (or the appearance of truth) in what postmodernists avow to make their dogma easy for the masses to believe and embrace. To be able to believe and do whatever you want is a very appealing doctrine, isn't it? However, the relativistic, pluralistic direction of postmodernity that many people in contemporary American

174

society have espoused (without much in the way of critical analysis) has not resulted in many positive benefits.

Even with all of modernity's shortcomings, America is rich and strong, and powerful and Americans enjoy many things because of the thinking made possible by modernity.

American society is a work in progress and how it will evolve (modern, postmodern, or some yet to be proposed alternative) is unclear. What is clear, however, is that Americans continue to work out of a basic Western worldview: naturalistic, rationalistic and individualistic, but also (for many) still spiritual, making room for God and faith and morality. It is a worldview that manifests itself in some very distinctive ways—which will be the subject of the next chapter.

Chapter 10

Why Are Americans the Way They Are

People from other cultural contexts observe Americans and wonder, *why are Americans like that?* In this chapter, we will consider some of the assumptions that are part of the American worldview and discuss how those underlying assumptions result in behavior characteristic of Western culture. A brief review of the material in chapter 1, along with some new material regarding worldview will be helpful as we proceed.

Worldview: Universals, Paradigms, Themes

Worldview is *the unconscious, deep-level assumptions people have about reality as they perceive it; assumptions about how the world works and how to relate to and interact with all the things, events and people encountered in life.* People acquire their worldview during childhood as they experience and observe, learn, and develop. These deep-level, underlying assumptions about reality become an interpretive filter through which people interpret and respond to all of life's experiences.

For instance, our worldview tells us what is important or not important, what is good or bad, right or wrong. From our assumptions about reality, we think about life either naturalistically or supernaturalistically, holistically or dichotomistically.

Worldview assumptions are rooted in the basic *Self-Other* concerns of life: how do I as *Self* relate to everything and everyone else in life as *Other*.

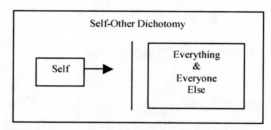

FIGURE 2: SELF-OTHER DICHOTOMY

Worldview assumptions, therefore, tell us how to think, for example, about relationships. Do we think and act as a person who is part of a group, or as an individual?

Universals

Researchers who specialize in worldview studies have analyzed these basic assumptions about life and found that they can be grouped into five categories called universals: *causality, classification, relationship, orientation to space, orientation to time.*

Causality—assumptions about why things happen, forces or powers in the cosmos that are somehow involved in the unfolding of day-to-day life. Are these forces or powers impersonal forces (such as gravity) beyond the influence of humans? Or are they personal beings whose choices and powers can be influenced by human beings? If the "forces" are impersonal forces beyond the influence of humans, how do we cope with the events they cause? If the "powers" are personal beings that humans can influence, how does one go

177

about influencing them in order to achieve the desired result? These are the kinds of questions/assumptions involved in the worldview universal of Causality.

Classification—assumptions about how things are related, how all things in life are categorized in relation to everything else. Why would some people put an orange, a chicken's foot and a monkey into the same category? Because for some people all three of those things are food. The way we classify people and things depends on our worldview assumptions. I would not classify my wife or children as part of the property I own. Many men from traditional societies would. In my way of classifying things that happen I have a category for "accidents" and another for "random occurrences." Many people in the world do not have an "accidents" or "random occurrences" category, because for them there are no such things as accidents or random occurrences. For those people, things happen because someone (perhaps God, or a spirit or an ancestor) made them happen.

Relationship—assumptions about our self and the kind of relationships we sustain with those around us. Am I first and foremost an individual whose primary identity and value grow out of my presence as an individual? Or am I first and foremost part of a group of people with my identity and value growing out of my relationship with and to that group? And do I view others primarily as individuals or as members of a group—either my group or not my group? If my assumptions about how life is to be lived are rooted in a group orientation, who is my group, that is, my family and who is not? Who is community and who is not? If my worldview assumptions are rooted in an individual orientation, what level of autonomy is required? How can I be an individual and still be part of a family group? Who comes first, the group or me? How does a group that is made up of "individuals" function differently than a group of people who are primarily members of a group? How are

178

decisions made? How are freedom and responsibility factored in? These kinds of *"how do I relate to other people?"* questions fall into the Relationship universal of worldview assumptions.

Orientation to space—assumptions related to how I think about the space I occupy, my relationship to the world, to nature, to things, my place in the world. Am I part of the space I occupy or separate from it? Do I own it, use it, manage it? Is there a space in the world that is mine or do I share all the space with other people? Do I share it with all other people or only with those who are my people? How should space (mine or ours) be organized? Should it be specialized and compartmentalized or used holistically? Should buildings be round or angular? Should there be private property or should there be community sharing of all resources? Does my orientation start with myself and go outward to other people and things, or does it begin outwardly with other people and things and move inward toward me?

For instance, a person with an orientation that starts with himself and goes outward who is walking from north to south and who passes a tree will think in terms of the tree as being on his right. His orientation is himself. He measures his world by himself, by his place in it. On his return walk, now going south, he will think in terms of the tree being on his left. This person thinks of the world (the space he occupies) from a *self-central focus*. He is the central focus. The world exists in relation to himself.

A person with a *world-central focus* making the same trips past the tree would think of the tree as the central feature, an enduring part of the bigger picture that is the point of reference rather than himself (Kearney 1983:161-164). A self-central-focus and a world-central-focus represent two very different orientations to the space we occupy, the world we live in.

179

Orientation to time—assumptions regarding how time works and how we think about it and use time. Is time like a river that flows out of the past, into the present and on into the future? Or is time like a circle of recurring events from season to season and generation to generation? If time can be compared to a tree, am I focused on the roots that reach into the past, on the trunk that is a substantial representation of the very solid present, or on the branches that reach up toward a future that is yet to unfold? Do I live my life with a past, present, or future orientation? Is life to be thought of as an ongoing series of events and relationships that occur as they unfold, moments that vary in duration and quality? Or is life to be viewed as moments to be calculated, organized, measured, and managed? Western people will answer these questions differently than non-Western people.

Which is the more important concern, what has happened in the past, or what may happen in the future? The present is real. The future is not yet real. How much of the present should I devote to an attempt to impact a future that is not yet real and that may not become real? Am I more concerned with the quality of an event and the relationships that are created or nourished by the event, or am I more concerned with the timeframe in which the events occur? Is it more important to be focused on where you are or where you are going to be? In the living of life and the passing of days are there relationships to be enjoyed or schedules to be kept? Is the passage of time equated with the quality of life or with productivity and profit?

Our Western orientation to time is not usually an all or nothing approach with punctually, for example, winning out over relationships. Most Americans will tell you that relationships are more important than punctuality. However, when you observe how they behave it is apparent that punctuality is often given priority over relationships. For example, a wife calls her husband at work to discuss a matter with him. He explains that he has a meeting in ten minutes and needs to pull together his notes and files. Can they discuss the matter later? Which was more important, talking to his wife or getting to the meeting fully prepared on time? The way Americans behave illustrates their true beliefs about time and how it is to be managed.

As you can see, each of these five worldview universal categories involves a number of significant and complex questions and issues that have serious implications for how we live life. Figure 3 is a diagram of worldview universals.

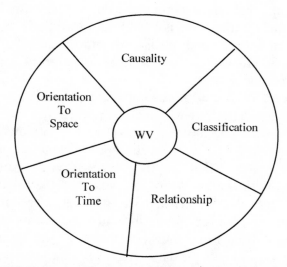

FIGURE 3: WORLDVIEW UNIVERSALS
WORLDVIEW AS A REALITY FILTER

Paradigms and Themes

Universals are the basic categories of assumptions people have about reality and how life ought to be lived. Growing out of each of those universals are other assumptions or categories of thinking about how the world works and how life is to be lived. These can be referred to as

181

paradigms. In the context of worldview, *a paradigm is a framework of concepts used as guidelines or parameters for further thinking about reality and how to live life.*

For instance, in the causality universal we deal with assumptions related to causes. Why do things happen, or who causes things to happen? Are the "forces" behind what happens in the material world, impersonal, the laws of physics, or personal, God or spirits. Or is there some combination—a personal God who is active in his world but who has established laws of physics by which the world operates as a rational, predictable, law abiding place, but in which God can still intervene and carry out his plans? Our assumptions about causality result in further assumptions about reality and how life is to be lived. This second tier of assumptions is what I am referring to as a paradigm. Each universal category will generate one or more paradigms in relation to it. The paradigms provide people with a framework for how their assumptions will be lived out in practical ways. The paradigmatic framework is lived out in a practical way in life *themes.*

In chapter 1, I described culture as a three-tired phenomenon made up 1) of our *deep-level* assumptions about the world and about how life is to be lived (called *worldview*), 2) of our *mid-level* internal values and our ways of feeling and thinking that grow out of our deep-level worldview assumptions, and 3) of our *surface-level* behaviors and structures. Figure 1 illustrates this phenomenon.

We can use this same framework for understanding the three-tired relationship between *universals, paradigms* and *themes.*

For instance, suppose a person believes in God who is active in his world, but who established physical laws to manage the cosmos. These assumptions occur at level-1, the deep *universal* level. Up one level would be the *paradigm* level, level-2. At this level, assumptions from level-1 are used to construct a framework for understanding the world

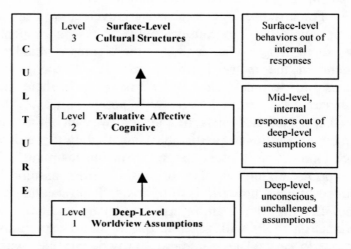

FIGURE 1: THREE-TIERED VIEW OF CULTURE

and living life in meaningful ways. Up another level, level-3, would be the *theme* level, the surface level where life is actually lived.

The person who believes that God is active in his world, but also established physical laws by which the universe operates holds these assumptions at the deep, universal level, level-1. This person's assumptions are both supernaturalistic and naturalistic. These assumptions from level-1 are used by the individual internally (and usually without conscious intent) to form a framework for how to live life in a meaningful way in relation to these assumptions. In other words, how does a person live who assumes the world is a place where both supernatural and natural forces are at work? These issues are worked out internally at the paradigm level, level-2. The results of internal operations that occur at the paradigm level are seen in the theme level, level-3, the surface level of life where one's assumptions are lived out in meaningful ways.

Assumptions at the universal level lead to a framework for living at the paradigm level which leads to the actual life themes that are lived out at the surface level. Let's stick with our person whose assumptions at the universal level are both supernaturalistic and naturalistic. Let's call this a SN universal, because of the combination of supernaturalistic and naturalistic assumptions. Both of these assumptions will be woven together at the paradigm level, resulting in a SN paradigm, that is, in a framework for living that will make it possible for the person to live according to his or her supernaturalistic and naturalistic assumptions. A person with a SN paradigm would be a person (at the theme level) of both faith *and* of science. When sick, this person would pray to God to be healed *and* take medicine. The supernaturalistic and naturalistic assumptions blended together at the paradigm level create surface-level behaviors (life themes) which are surface-level manifestations of one's deep-level assumptions about the nature of the world and how life is to be lived. Figure 4 illustrates the process in diagram form.

This very technical (and yet only partial) explanation of how worldview works is necessary if we are to understand why Americans are the way they are.

Typical Western Worldview Assumptions

Discussing "typical" Western or American worldview assumptions is a challenge because generalizations of any kind, when you are talking about humans, are tricky. Whose list of "typical" are we going to go by, yours, mine, or someone else's?

184

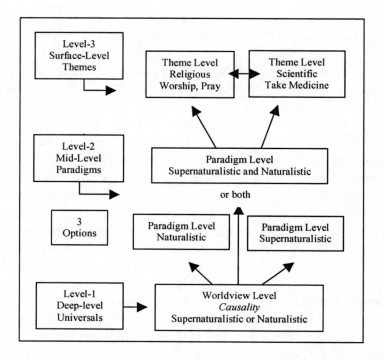

FIGURE 4: UNIVERSALS, PARADIGMS, THEMES

Having acknowledged the challenge of "typical," I believe it is possible to think in terms of a typical or basic Western worldview—as long as we understand that we are discussing (in the broadest possible strokes) the deep-level, underlying assumptions most basically characteristic of the Western worldview[9]. We are not thinking in terms of a list

[9] It is important to keep in mind that the "American" worldview assumptions I will discuss in this section are not entirely unique to Americans. Many European cultures also share a number of these same assumptions. Also, many people from non-Western cultures share many of these same assumptions to varying degrees due to the widespread influence of Western culture since the end of World War II. The process of globalization has resulted in the "westernization" of many non-Western, non-Enlightenment driven cultures.

of activities or behaviors in which Americans engage. We are thinking in terms of underlying worldview assumptions that ultimately generate certain behaviors. But our focus is not on the behaviors; it is on the assumptions that underlie the behaviors.

Not all Americans share a common worldview. There will always be some variation, especially between sub-cultural groups or ethnic minority populations and the dominant population group—Anglos. Obviously, when I speak of *Americans* and the *American worldview*, I am referring to a very basic social grouping where a number of individuals share some common assumptions. We can't get too picky here. We're going to look at a big picture that is painted in very broad strokes. To do this we will think in terms of the five universal worldview categories.

Causality

Americans assume that the cosmos is governed by physical laws and operates in a rational, law-abiding way. Whether they think of the cosmos as a machine or an organism, it works in an orderly, predictable way. It can be studied, understood, engaged and manipulated. Americans assume a cause and effect framework. If I drop a book it falls to the floor. The book falling to the floor is the effect. The cause is the law of gravity. A headache is the effect of some internal cause—perhaps insufficient blood flow because of constricted muscles in the upper back and neck because of too much stress. The headache can be impacted by medication—chemicals that interact with the nervous system to minimize the pain. There is a cause and an effect, another cause and another effect.

Because Americans assume the universe is a rational, orderly, law-abiding place that can be studied, understood, engaged, and manipulated, they assume that they, too, must be rational in the way they think about and study the

186

universe. The universe is not chaotic, so thinking should not be chaotic. Orderly, logical, predictable: to function in that kind of a world we must have that kind of a mind and live that kind of a life. This is the naturalistic, rationalistic (scientific) part of a typical American worldview.

But many Americans also assume the existence a God who is (to some extent) active in his world. He cares about his human children and is present and active in the lives of those who seek him out. He listens to and answers prayer. He created humans in his image and wants to enjoy a relationship with them. He is a moral and just God who requires his human offspring to be moral and just. Therefore, for many Americans, moral absolutes exist. The need to be truthful and honest guides them in their dealings with others.

There is another segment of the American population that believes in some form of power or intelligence that exists on a spiritual plane. They do not have a well-formulated or articulated theology about a personal God with whom one can enjoy a relationship, but they do have some vague ideas about the importance of spirituality and broadly accepted standards of right and wrong. Organized religion does not interest them, but they are moral, ethical people.

Historically, America has been a Christian nation. Many of the laws that govern us are rooted in the Judeo-Christian traditions that are 4,000 to 2,000 years old. The morals and ethics that were preached from pulpits were also passed on from generation to generation within a strong family context. Those same morals and ethics were echoed in schools, colleges, and universities for several generations. Only recently have some institutions and segments within our society advocated a relinquishing of the Judeo-Christian values that made our nation strong.

In that social context, where Judeo-Christian values were the social norm, even people who were not religious and did not attend church services were educated and trained within a broad moral, ethical, and social framework that was fundamentally Judeo-Christian.

Most Americans, then, in the early 21st century, have a worldview that, as far as the causality universal is concerned, is both naturalistic and supernaturalistic. Americans, generally speaking, are people of science and people of faith.

Many Americans have concluded that science can't answer all of life's questions (especially the most interesting ones), but many important issues can be investigated and understood by rigorous scientific inquiry. Scientific discoveries can improve and prolong life and Americans are interested in both of those. Issues that aren't subject to scientific inquiry are just as important and many Americans give considerable time and attention to the pursuit of spiritual concerns.

Classification

Classification is probably the most difficult universal to discuss in relation to a group of people. Talking about how Americans classify things is nearly impossible so this will be very general. Perhaps the best way to approach the subject is to discuss a few of the classification categories that exist for Americans and allow readers to compare those categories with their own.

Americans have a number of classification categories that are consistent with the assumptions they have in other universals. For instance, because most Americans have a naturalistic, mechanistic view of the world, they believe in accidents and random occurrences. An unintended result is an accident. If I unintentionally knock over a glass of water, spilling the water onto the table, that is an accident. Most Americans believe in accidental occurrences—things happening that no one intended to happen. Many people in the world do not believe in accidents. For them, everything happens because someone makes it happen. Those people have no classification category in their thinking for accidents.

For most Americans, the destruction wrought by a tornado or hurricane would not qualify as accident. The development of a tornado or hurricane are the direct results of a series of physical interactions that are, to a degree, predictable. Specific weather conditions result in a tornado or a hurricane. However, for most Americans, the path a tornado takes, moving this way or that, jumping from one place to another, changing direction suddenly, would be considered a random occurrence. In fact, even the development of the specific weather conditions that result in a tornado or hurricane would, for most Americans, be considered a random occurrence.

However, many Americans also have a category related to their supernatural assumptions, a category of classification that allows for God to act in his world. Some events are accidents, some are random occurrences, some are divine intervention. God responds to prayer, and God has a grand design he is busy administering. Some events are classified as natural, some as supernatural. Some Americans have a thoughtful and thorough method for decided which events are natural and which are supernatural, while others do not. But for most Americans, both kinds of classifications exist.

Americans classify personal space differently than some other groups of people. Most Americans consider the 30 inches around them to be their personal space. If someone other than a child or spouse invades the personal space of an American he or she gets uncomfortable and will move in an attempt to adjust the space to the appropriate distance. Americans do not appreciate people crowding too close to them while standing in line or sitting too close on a bench or on a bus or train. Personal space is a serious classification issue for Americans.

Many Americans have more classification categories than some other people groups, because Americans (and Western people in general) think dichotomistically rather than holistically. This is due to the influence of science and the precise, categorical thinking that is necessary to conduct research and analyze and record data. The more a people tend to analyze things the more categories they have for classifying the things they analyze.

Americans, then, because they think about life dichotomistically, have lots of categories for classification. They tend to be very precise. Personal space is an important classification for Americans and most Americans have classification categories for accidents and random occurrences.

Relationship

Americans are first and foremost individuals. Americans belong to many different kinds of groups: family, church, clubs, associations, teams, political parties, study groups, hobby groups, social activist groups, protest groups and so forth. But regardless of how many groups Americans belong to, Americans (especially Anglos) are individuals before they are anything else. Even family concerns come after individual concerns. Americans are autonomous rational individuals who matter just because they exist, who have certain rights simply because they are human beings. Relationships are important to Americans. Other people are important to Americans. But nothing is more important (for most Americans) than their own personal sense of being. Descartes' datum of indisputable truth might be extended to, *I think, therefore I am, therefore I matter*.

It is this overpowering and all-pervasive sense of self that impacts and drives so much of American life on a day-to-day basis. Decisions are made individually, not collectively. Priorities are set based on individual needs and

190

interests. Even the rights guaranteed by American governing documents are the rights of the individual.

America is a nation of individuals—individuals who believe in the pursuit of excellence, progress, achievement, success. And they believe in pursuing those things so strongly—as individuals—that relationships with others often suffer from neglect or are considered less important.

Because Americans are so individualistic, they spend less time building and maintaining relationships than other peoples. Many Americans (especially Anglo males) would rather spend thirty minutes being productive as an individual than spend thirty minutes nurturing a relationship.

The individualistic spirit that dominates the American psyche, combined with a strong sense of personal responsibility and a guilt-justice perspective on social control, leads many Americans to utilize (to a degree) a confrontational method of dealing with conflict. Teamwork is important. But often individuals on the team are recognized for outstanding achievement. Major American sports (football, baseball, basketball) recognize the MVP— Most Valuable Player: individual recognition in a team sport.

Americans are first and foremost, individuals.

Orientation to Space

One's orientation to space has to do with the assumptions one has regarding his or her relationship with or to the space one occupies. Americans tend to think in terms of ownership. The space around an American is his or her space. If you get too close to an American (closer than 30 inches), unless you are a spouse or a child, you are invading his or her personal space. But the American orientation to space involves considerably more than just a few inches of personal space.

On a cosmic scale, *space* (in an anthropological worldview universal sense of the term) has to do with the

191

physical world in which one lives; it has to do with one's relationship to nature and everything with which one comes in contact. Americans typically see themselves as separate from nature. Americans know that they are part of the cosmos. They are part of the whole. Yet, at the same time, most Americans see themselves (at least they act like they see themselves) as somehow separate from it, above it. The cosmos is there to be explored, discovered, understood, used, enjoyed, managed, manipulated. If American behavior is the gauge, Americans believe the world was created for them, to meet their needs, for their use. They are to be responsible in managing it, but it is there for human use and enjoyment.

On a more personal scale, Americans think the space they occupy in terms of property they own and need to arrange. In our discussion of classification, I noted that Americans tend to analyze everything and so they have categories for everything they analyze. American thinking is dichotomized and compartmentalized, and so is the day-to-day life of the typical American. We live in houses that have specialized rooms—rooms for sleeping, for eating, for storing cars and tools, rooms for bathing and the elimination of biological waste, rooms for cooking and general use rooms for relaxation and entertainment, rooms for storing clothing and items for use in the house.

This specialized compartmentalization of space is serious business for Americans. The multi-billion dollar home repair/maintenance/decoration/remodeling industry exist so individuals and families can care for and further specialize their compartmentalized living space. For American children, it is a badge of honor to have one's own room (bedroom) rather than having to share with other siblings. Parents take great pride in having the financial resources to purchase a home large enough so each child can have his or her own room—especially by the time they are teenagers. Even infants often have their own separate rooms—a practice that some other cultures find horrible, because in their view very young children should not be isolated from their parents.

Americans privatize, personalize, compartmentalize and specialize *their* space. The American orientation to space is closely connected to their deep appreciation of individualism.

Orientation to Time

Americans are future oriented. The past is the past. It is what it is and there's nothing that can be done about it. The present, also, is what it is. Little can be done to impact the present moment. But the future, the future is coming and if one engages in strategic planning and activity, the future can be shaped and molded to provide a more advantageous set of circumstances. Americans plan for retirement. Americans plan for the education of their children. Americans plan their career. They plan their vacation. They plan to remodel their home, to buy a new car. They plan and schedule activities and events days, weeks, and even months in advance.

Americans plan and plan and plan, because the future is coming and it will be here before you know it. And there is never enough time to get everything done. For most Americans, time is a commodity to be used wisely, frugally. Time is one of the few things you can't make more of. So what you have must be carefully allocated.

Because Americans are focused on progress (one of the fundamental goals of modernism) they are also focused on productivity. The two concepts are linked. Productivity is also a major factor of a capitalistic economic system. The more you make the more you have to sell, the more you have to sell the greater potential for profit. But it is not just making a lot of a thing. It is making it making it efficiently and inexpensively. Time factors into the whole process of productivity. It is part of the production cost equation. It is this connection between productivity and time that causes Americans to see time as money. Thus the saying, *time is money.*

To people from Non-Western cultures, Americans seem obsessed with time. We wear watches or carry PDAs or phones with us so we can check the time. We have clocks in nearly every room in our home. Businesses are run by the clock; schools are run by the clock; hospitals are run by the clock; churches are run by the clock. Our cars have clocks in them; our televisions have clocks in them.

Time is related to productivity, to progress, to efficiency. The better we manage time the more efficient we are. The more efficient we are the more we get done. The more we get done the more productive we are. The more productive we are the more successful we are. The more successful we are the better we are. The better we are the more progress we are making. And, well, progress is what it is all about. Forward and upward—to infinity and beyond!

What all this translates into on a practical level is that Americans are very serious about punctuality. If a meeting is scheduled for 9:00 AM it begins at 9:00 AM not 9:05 AM. People who are late are considered undisciplined, rude and perhaps even lazy. From an American point of view, if you are supposed to be somewhere at 8:00 AM, get up early enough so you can do everything you need to do and be where you are supposed to be at 8:00 AM. Kids are not a valid excuse. Neither is traffic. Manage your life and manage your time and be where you are supposed to be when you are supposed to be there. It's the American way.

Ideas Americans Value

The very broad and general assumptions that make up a people's worldview, as we have seen, develop into ideas that people cherish, which in turn are expressed in cultural behaviors. We have discussed some of the assumptions that

194

are part of the Western (and therefore American) worldview. It might be helpful to think in terms of some of the ideas Americans hold dear. In doing this I am not attempting to follow the development of assumptions into paradigms into themes that I diagrammed earlier in this chapter. Instead, I'm just presenting a few ideas Americans hold dear and which impact their behavior.

In *American Cultural Patterns*, Edward Stewart and Milton Bennett, in discussing assumptions and values note that, "middle-class Americans usually think of themselves as individuals, the world as inanimate, other people as competitive but capable of cooperation, and action as necessary for survival," (1991:13). Though not anthropologists and not using worldview assumptions as a framework for their discussion, Stewart and Bennett are discussing the same idea, illustrating how cultural behaviors grow out of cultural assumptions and values.

Along similar lines, Joann Crandall, Maryanne Kearney Datesman and Edward N. Kearney note what they refer to as "six basic values" of American culture. These are: *individual freedom, self-reliance, equality of opportunity, competition, material wealth, and hard work* (1997:29).

I like their list. Let's consider each concept briefly.

Individual Freedom

The need to be free grows out of the idea that each person is an autonomous rational individual. If that is in fact the case, then freedom—freedom to think, to decide, and to act in one's own best interest—is intrinsic in humans. If the individual is to thrive there must be freedom. Where there is no freedom there is no individual pursuing his or her potential as a person.

Americans have fought and died for freedom because they are autonomous rational individuals who are going to be free—no matter what. So when the founding fathers drew up the documents that articulated the principles by which the nation would be governed very specific language was used to safeguard fundamental human freedoms. Americans are committed to the idea of individual freedom.

Self-reliance

If a person is an autonomous individual, and if that person is to be free, he or she must be self-reliant. To be dependent on others minimizes one's own freedom. Young people know this. When you live in your parent's home you live by their rules. Freedom is limited. The more independent one is the more self-reliant he or she must be.

In the kind of society we live in no one is completely self-reliant. We don't hunt our own food and make our own clothes from the skins of the animals we kill and eat. We don't grow our own vegetables. We don't drill our own oil to refine into gasoline to put in the car we built ourselves. We live in an interdependent society. We sell our time and skills for a paycheck so we can buy the things we need from other people. Self-reliance in 21st century America means something different than it meant in the 18th century. But within the framework of an interdependent society, Americans enjoy being as independent and self-reliant as they can be.

Self-reliance is so important to Americans that they are willing to pay the high price associated with it. Young people venture out on their own, often before they are emotionally or financially prepared, because they want to be self-reliant. Senior citizens refuse to relinquish the independence and self-reliance they have enjoyed all their adult lives, preferring instead to live alone rather than be taken care of by their children—even when their physical condition makes self-reliance difficult.

An interesting social observation related to self-reliance has to do with ethnic gang activity. Very seldom does one encounter Anglo gangs. Why is that? Because self-reliance is a fundamental feature of the Anglo heart and mind. Anglo children are taught self-reliance. A man stands on his own two feet and he stands alone. If he can't, he isn't much of a man. Sometimes it's a hard way of life. But most Anglos feel the benefits outweigh the cost.

Equality of Opportunity

One of the reasons European immigrants began pouring to this country in the 18th and 19th centuries and continue to come today is because America is the *land of opportunity*. Status in America (generally speaking) is earned, not ascribed. The person who works smart and hard, regardless of social status, can achieve a level of success that is not possible in other cultural contexts.

In Europe, where most of the immigrants came from in the 18th and 19th centuries, there was a ruling class, a wealthy aristocracy that enjoyed benefits of opportunity. The poorer classes did not have access to opportunity. For the most part, one's station in life was fixed at birth and only the most extraordinary circumstances could open doors of opportunity. But in America the doors of opportunity were open to anyone with the courage and tenacity to step through them. Courageous, tenacious people did step through those doors. They came and they built. They excelled; they achieved. Courageous, tenacious people are still coming for the same reason: opportunity.

Americans respect people who work smart and hard. Part of working smart is getting an education, learning how to think, how to speak and how to present oneself effectively. Working smart also means working honestly: telling the truth, keeping your word, paying taxes, working within the system according to the rules. Working hard means working long hours, doing what it takes to succeed. The person digging a ditch in the hot sun is working hard.

197

But so is the person sitting at the computer 16 hours a day marketing his or her product or service.

There is a lot of debate in some circles whether or not all Americans really do enjoy equal opportunity. A few people do not think so. But I believe most Americans believe that everyone has the opportunity to build a good life if they work smart and hard.

Competition

If you take a big group of autonomous rational individuals who crave self-reliance and want to make the most of the opportunities they have to build something for themselves and their families, what do you get? Competition. Fierce competition. In some cultural contexts competition is a bad thing. Americans thrive on competition. Capitalism requires an atmosphere of free market competition. America is a capitalistic culture of competitors.

Children are taught to compete. American children compete scholastically, athletically, and socially. There are few areas of American life that are not touched by competition. Americans love to win and Americans love winners. That's why Americans say things like, *if a game's worth playing it's worth winning.* The ancient Greeks invented the Olympic athletic competition because they loved to compete. As the West evolved into a capitalistic competitive society, Europeans reinvented the Olympics as a celebration of the competitive spirit and the drive to be the best. People who succeed, who excel, who achieve in America will be people with a competitive spirit who want to be the best they can be at what they do and at who they are.

Material wealth

How does one measure success in a competitive, capitalistic society? By wealth. Why is it necessary to

198

measure? Because the nature of competition requires it. If there's going to be competition, there has to be a way to measure the outcome. In a race, the one who crosses the finish line first is the winner. But the race of life can't be judged that way. So how do we measure success in life? For many Americans, the measure is material wealth: living in a nice house, driving a nice car, wearing nice clothes, eating in nice restaurants, sending your children to a prestigious school, taking nice vacations.

Many Americans, however, have begun to wonder whether material wealth is, in fact, a valid measure of success. If material wealth is one's goal then the accumulation of wealth would be an appropriate measure. However, if one's goal is to be happy and relaxed, doing what one enjoys, then material wealth may not be an appropriate indicator of success. Still, many Americans have been conditioned to equate success with wealth. America is, whether we like to admit it or not, a very materialistic nation. We work, work, work, to earn, earn, earn to spend, spend, spend, to have, have, have. We are forever in pursuit of happiness, believing it lies just beyond the next purchase.

Hard work

Competitive people who want to be successful work hard. That's the key. Luck sometimes becomes a factor— being in the right place at the right time with the right idea, product or service. But most people who have "made it" will tell you that you make your own luck, you make your own breaks. What about those people who have worked hard all their lives and still haven't made it? For the people who have made it, who have succeeded, it is understood that *working hard* also means *working smart*. Either one without the other is a waste of time. Working hard without working smart doesn't guarantee success.

Individualistic, self-reliant Americans do not believe that the government should take care of people. People should work hard to take care of themselves. Lots of people hit a rough spot in the road and need help. Americans believe in helping each other—to a degree. If a person trips and falls, Americans will extend a helping hand and get him back on his feet. But if the person who has fallen prefers to lie on the ground whining about his misfortune. . . well, the helping hand is only going to be extended for a short period of time. Self-reliant people expect others to be self-reliant as well. Hard working people expect others to be hard working too. In America, hard work is what it takes to succeed.

Summary

The *American worldview* can only be discussed in the broadest possible terms. There is a great deal of worldview variation between different groups of Americans, especially in some areas. However, having granted that, generally speaking, it is possible to identify and discuss a general Western worldview in broad strokes.

Beginning with worldview universals we can say that generally speaking Americans assume naturalistic and supernaturalistic causes in the universe and are both people of science and people of faith. Americans have lots of classification categories that are consistent with other worldview assumptions. They have categories for accidents and random events; they classify occurrences sometimes as natural, sometimes as supernatural.

Relationally, Americans are individualistic. Americans belong to many different groups, but each person is first and foremost an individual following his or her own course in life.

As for their orientation to space, Americans tend to think in terms of ownership and management. They are part of the world they live in, yet also separate from it. Most

200

Americans have a *self-central focus*. Americans take their personal space seriously and don't like it when it is invaded. Their personal space, be it car, office, home, or room within the home is compartmentalized and personalized.

The American orientation to time is rooted in the future and requires serious management because time is limited and must be managed wisely in order to allow for maximum productivity.

Ideas Americans values because of their worldview assumptions include individual freedom, self-reliance, equal opportunity, competition, material wealth and hard work.

There are lots of other things that make Americans they way they are, but these are some of the most basic.

Conclusion

Our journey has been a long one. We began by developing a theoretical framework for thinking about our journey and destination—worldview as the foundation of culture. To understand American culture we must understand the American worldview, a worldview with roots in the ancient Middle East of 4,000 years ago and ancient Greece of 2,500 years ago. The foundational concepts that emerged from ancient Judaism were carried into and blended with Christian traditions, to create the Judeo-Christian tradition. The Judeo-Christian tradition has exerted as much influence on the development of Western civilization as any other single force. The religion, theology, and spirituality of the Judeo-Christian tradition have been and continue to be dynamic forces shaping Western morals, ethics, laws, and social norms.

Another force that has been as formative in the development of Western civilization (and therefore of America) as the Judeo-Christian tradition is ancient Greek philosophy and the Western philosophical traditions that evolved from it during the Renaissance and Enlightenment. The rediscovery of classical philosophy in the late Middle Ages led to the development of Scholasticism which created a new kind of scholarship and allowed for the consideration of new perspectives. Those emerging perspectives blossomed into the Renaissance, laying the foundation for the Enlightenment.

Pre-Enlightenment philosophy laid the foundation for the development of a philosophical-scientific way of thinking about the cosmos that changed the West. Christians struggled with new and old ways of thinking. Powerful church leaders with minds darkened by fears of the unknown tried to stem the tide of change. But as the literal tide of the sea cannot be stopped, neither could the newly awakened curiosity of the human mind set free. Ideas emerged. Exploration, experimentation, and enlightenment enveloped the Western world and it would never be the same again.

The discovery of physical laws that govern the universe, which can be studied and understood, led to a view of the world as part of a cosmic machine, a mechanistic world that could be understood with mathematical precision.

With a new view of the cosmos came a new view of humankind, a Christian humanist view. In this mechanistic world each person was an autonomous rational individual. Rational minds would study the rational world and with the knowledge acquired progress would be made, astonishing progress that would one day solve cosmic riddles, and rid the world of hunger and suffering. What a future! A new world had arrived, a modern world. Modernity was born and the modern project was underway.

The new philosophical perspective was powerful and there were some anti-Christian sentiments involved, especially as Christian humanism gave way to secular humanism. For some (mostly hard core philosophers or other academics) spiritual concerns were relegated to the realm of the superstitious. But for the average person religion and spiritual concerns remained significant. They would not relinquish the theological in order to grasp the philosophical. In one hand they held their spiritual beliefs, in the other they held new philosophical ideas. Unwilling to abandon either, many Western people found ways of combining the two. They became people of faith and of science, making them unique in the world.

It was that blending of the Judeo-Christian heritage and the new philosophical perspective that lent itself so effectively to the development of new political ideology so firmly grounded in moral absolutes and Christian ethics. It was the blending of Judeo-Christian theology and Enlightenment philosophy that allowed for the evolution of thought that resulted in the founding of the United States of America.

That same theological/philosophical blending continues to impact the American people today. Although hardcore Enlightenment philosophy challenged the existence of God and the validity of spiritual pursuits, the presence of Judeo-Christian principles as powerful underlying features of Western culture would not be diminished. Even the subtle and pervasive presence of postmodern philosophy has not been able to minimize the powerful presence of the Judeo-Christian perspective.

If we think specifically about the theological and philosophical forces that shape the American worldview, and therefore the American people, it is possible to develop a short list for each category.

Broadly speaking, what are the Judeo-Christian influences that have impacted American thinking and behavior?

1. Monotheism.
2. Moral absolutes.
3. A guilt-justice orientation.
4. The rule of law carried out in lower and higher courts.
5. A Golden Rule approach to life.
6. Moral integrity as evidenced in honesty, personal growth and personal responsibility.

Broadly speaking, what are the philosophical influences of modernism that have impacted American thinking and behavior?

1. A naturalistic focus.
2. A strong individualistic orientation.
3. Rationalism.
4. A scientific paradigm with a mechanistic view of the cosmos.

Broadly speaking, what are the philosophical influences of postmodernism that have impacted American thinking and behavior?

1. An increased focus on subjectivity and relativity.
2. A concern that ultimate truth and moral absolutes may not exist.
3. An almost militaristic demand for pluralism—the only belief that is not acceptable is the belief that not everything is acceptable.

Obviously these short lists are not exhaustive. But they do represent significant influences that have impacted American thinking and behavior. The unique blend of Judeo-Christian tradition and Greek philosophical thinking (filtered and refined during the Renaissance and Enlightenment) have created a unique American perspective. It is that unique way of thinking about and living life that makes Americans who they are.

Works Cited

Adkins, Lesley and Roy A. Adkins
    1994   *Handbook to Life in Ancient Rome*. New York: Oxford.

Barna Group, The
    2006   Church Attendance.
    http://www.barna.org/FlexPage.aspx?Page=Topic&TopicID=10

Beaud, Michel
    2001   *A History of Capitalism: 1500-2000*. New York:
    Monthly Review Press.

Blackwell, C.W.
    2003   "Athenian Democracy: A Brief Overview," in C.
    Blackwell, ed. *Demos: Classical Athenian Democracy*. A.
    Mahoney and R. Scaife, edd., The Stoa: a consortium for
    electronic publication in the humanities, www.stoa.org
    http://www.stoa.org/projects/demos/home

Bowra, C. M.
    1965   *Classical Greece*. Alexandria: Time-Life.

Braunstein, Philippe
    1988   "Toward Intimacy: The Fourteenth and Fifteenth
    Centuries," in *A History of Private Life: Revelations of the
    Medieval World*. Georges Duby, ed. Cambridge: Belknap Press.

Brittan, Gordon G.
    1999   "Enlightenment," in *The Cambridge Dictionary of
    Philosophy*. Robert Audi, ed. Cambridge: Cambridge
    University Press.

Brown, Colin
    1990   *Christianity and Western Thought: A History of
    Philosophers, Ideas and Movements, Volume 1, From the
    Ancient World to the Age of Enlightenment*. Downers Grove:
    InterVarsity Press.

Byrne, James M.
    1996   *Religion and the Enlightenment: From Descartes to
    Kant*. Louisville: Westminster.

Cahill, Thomas
    2003   *Sailing The Wine-Dark Sea: Why The Greeks Matter*.
    New York: Doubleday.

Cantor, Norman F.
  1994   *The Civilization of the Middle Ages.* New York: Harper
  Collins.

Carrithers, Michael
  1997   "Culture," in *The Dictionary of Anthropology.* Thomas
  Barfield, ed. Malden, Blackwell.

Cassirer, Ernst
  1979   *The Philosophy of the Enlightenment.* Princeton:
  Princeton University Press.

Chadwick, Henry
  1992   "The Early Christian Community," in *The Oxford
  Illustrated History of Christianity.* John McManners, ed.
  Oxford: Oxford.

  1993   *The Early Church: The Story of Emergent Christianity
  from the Apostolic Age to the Dividing of the Ways Between the
  Greek East and the Latin West.* England: Penguin.

Collins, Michael and Matthew A. Price
  2003   *The Story of Christianity: 2000 Years of Faith.* New
  York: DK Publishing.

Collinson, Patrick
  2000   "Reformation," in *The Oxford Companion to Christian
  Thought.* Adrian Hastings, ed. Oxford: Oxford.

Crandall, Joann, Maryanne Kearney Datesman and Edward N. Kearney
  1997   *The American Ways: An Introduction to American
  Culture.* White Plaines: Longman.
Cranston, Maurice
  1967   "Bacon, Francis," in *The Encyclopedia of Philosophy.*
  Paul Edwards, ed. New York: McMillan.

Dawson, Christopher
  1950   *Religion and the Rise of Western Culture.* New York:
  Doubleday.

DeMar, Gary
  2003   *America's Christian Heritage.* Nashville: Broadman and
  Holman.

Duby, Georges
  1988   *A History of Private Life: Revelations of the Medieval World*. Georges Duby, ed. Cambridge: Belknap Press.

Eidsmoe, John
  1987   *Christianity and the Constitution: The Faith of Our Founding Fathers*. Grand Rapids: Baker.

Ferguson, Everett
  1967   "A History of Palestine from the Fifth Century B.C. to the Second Century A.D.," in *The World of the New Testament*. Abraham J. Malherbe, ed. Austin: Sweet.

  1993   *Backgrounds of Early Christianity*. Grand Rapids: Eerdmans.

Feinberg, C. L.
  1998   "Synagogue," in *The Illustrated Bible Dictionary*. J. D. Douglas, ed. Downers Grove: InterVarsity.

Forrester, Duncan
  2000   "Justice," in *The Oxford Companion to Christian Thought*. Adrian Hastings, ed. Oxford: Oxford.

Freeman, Charles
  1996   *Egypt, Greece and Rome: Civilizations of the Ancient Mediterranean*. Oxford: Oxford.

  1999   *The Greek Achievement: The Foundation of the Western World*. New York: Viking.

Frost, S. E. Jr.
  1962   *Basic Teachings of the Great Philosophers*. New Books.

Grant, Michael
  1991   *The Founders of the Western World: A History of Greece and Rome*. New York: Scribner's.

Grayling, A. C.
  1995   "Modern Philosophy II: The Empiricists," in *Philosophy: A Guide through the Subject*. A.C. Grayling ed. Oxford: Oxford.

Grenz, Stanley J.
  1996   *A Primer on Postmodernism*. Grand Rapids: Eerdmans.

Hare, John
    2000 "Kant, Immanuel," in *The Oxford Companion to Christian Thought*. Adrian Hastings, ed. Oxford: Oxford.

Hinson, E. Glenn
    1996 *The Early Church: Origins to the Dawn of the Middle Ages*. Nashville: Abingdon.

Hiebert, Paul G.
    1983 *Cultural Anthropology*. Grand Rapids: Baker.

    1996 "The Gospel in Our Culture: Methods of Social and Cultural Analysis," in *The Church Between Gospel and Culture: The Emerging Mission in North America*. George Hunsberger and Craig Van Gelder, eds. Grand Rapids: Eerdmans.

    1999 *Missiological Implications of Epistemological Shifts: Affirming Truth in a Modern/Postmodern World*. Harrisburg: Trinity.

Hollis, Martin
    1985 *Invitation to Philosophy*. Cambridge: Blackwell.

Hutson, James H.
    1998 *Religion and the Founding of the American Republic*. Washington: Library of Congress.

Irvin, Dale T. and Scott W. Sunquist
    2001 *History of the World Christian Movement*. Maryknoll: Orbis.

Jacob, Margaret C.
    2001 *The Enlightenment: A Brief History with Documents*. Boston: St. Martins.

Johnson, Paul
    2003 *The Renaissance: A Short History*. New York: The Modern Library.

Kane, Herbert J.
    1982 *A Concise History of the Christian World Mission: A Panoramic View of Missions from Pentecost to the Present*. Grand Rapids: Baker.

Karney, Michael
    1984 *World View*. Novato: Chandler & Sharp.

Kenny, Anthony
1998 *A Brief History of Western Philosophy*. Malden: Blackwell.

Kerferd, G. B.
1967 "Aristotle," in *The Encyclopedia of Philosophy*. Paul Edwards, ed. New York: McMillan.

Kidd, I. G.
1967 "Socrates," in *The Encyclopedia of Philosophy*. Paul Edwards, ed. New York: McMillan.

Kosmin, Barry A. and Seymore P. Lachman
1993 *One Nation Under God: Religion in Contemporary American Society*. New York: Crown.

Kraft, Charles H.
1996 *Anthropology For Christian Witness*. Maryknoll: Orbis.

2002 *Worldview For Christian Witness*. Prepublication edition.

Kramnick, Isaac
1995 *The Portable Enlightenment Reader*. Isaac Kramnick, ed. New York: Penguin.

Kuhn, Thomas S.
1985 *The Copernican Revolution: Planetary Astronomy in the Development of Western Thought*. Cambridge: Harvard University Press.

Le Goff, Jacques
1988 *Medieval Civilization 400-1500*. New York: Barnes and Noble.

Martin, Ralph P.
1975 *New Testament Foundations: A Guide for Christian Students*, Vol. 1. Grand Rapids: Eerdmans.

Mason, Alistair
2000 "Enlightenment," in the *Oxford Companion to Christian Thought*. Adrian Hastings, ed. Oxford: Oxford.

210

Mayr-Harting, Henry
　　　　1990　"The West: The Age of Conversion," in *The Oxford Illustrated History of Christianity*. Oxford: Oxford University Press.

　　　　2001　"The Early Middle Ages," in *Christianity: Two Thousand Years*. Richard Harris and Henry Mayr-Harting, ed. Oxford: Oxford University Press.

McKelvey, R. J.
　　　　1998　"Temple," in *The Illustrated Bible Dictionary*. J. D. Douglas, ed. Downers Grove: InterVarsity.

Meyers, Eric M.
　　　　1992　"Synagogue," in *The Anchor Bible Dictionary*. David Freedman, ed. New York: Doubleday.

Mori, Anne and David Jessel
　　　　1991　*Brain Sex: The Real Difference Between Men and Women*. New York: Delta

Murray, Alexander
　　　　2001　"The Later Middle Ages," in *Christianity: Two Thousand Years*. Richard Harries and Henry Mayr-Harting, eds. Oxford: Oxford.

Oliver, Martyn
　　　　1999　*History of Philosophy*. New York: Barnes and Noble.

Oster, Richard, Jr.
　　　　1993　"Corinth," in *The Oxford Companion to the Bible*. Bruce Metzger and Michael Coogan, eds. New York: Oxford.

Punton, Anne
　　　　2002　*The World Jesus Knew*. Chicago: Moody.

Rice, Eugene F. and Anthony Grafton
　　　　1994　*The Foundations of Early Modern Europe, 1460-1559*. New York: W. W. Norton.

Roberts, Richard H.
　　　　2000　"Capitalism," in *The Oxford Companion to Christian Thought*. Adrian Hastings, ed. Oxford: Oxford.

Rogers, Glenn
    2002 *The Role of Worldview in Missions and Multiethnic Ministry*. Bedford: Mission and Ministry Resources.

    2006 *Evangelizing Immigrants: Outreach and Ministry Among Immigrants and Their Children*. Bedford: Mission and Ministry Resources.

Rubenstein, Richard E.
    2003 *Aristotle's Children: How Christians, Muslims, and Jews Rediscovered Ancient Wisdom and Illuminated the Dark Ages*. New York: Harcourt.

Ryle, Gilbert,
    1967 "Plato," in *The Encyclopedia of Philosophy*. Paul Edwards, ed. New York: McMillan

Scruton, Roger
    1995 "Modern Philosophy I: The Rationalists and Kant," in *Philosophy: A Guide through the Subject*. A. C. Grayling, ed. Oxford: Oxford.

Selman, M. J.
    1998 "House," in *The Illustrated Bible Dictionary*. J. D. Douglas, ed. Downers Grove: InterVarsity.

Sørensen, Preben Meulengracht
    1997 "Religions Old and New," in *The Oxford Illustrated History of the Vikings*. Peter Sawyer, ed. Oxford: Oxford University Press.

Southern, R. W.
    1990 *Western Society and the Church in the Middle Ages*. England: Penguin.

Spickard, Paul R. and Kevin M. Cragg
    1994 *A Global History of Christians: How Everyday Believers Experienced Their World*. Grand Rapids: Baker.

Starr, Chester G.
    1991 *A History of the Ancient World*. New York: Oxford.

Stewart, Edward C. and Milton J. Bennett
    1991 *American Cultural Patterns: A Cross-cultural Perspective*. Yarmouth: Intercultural Press.

212

Strangroom, Jeremy and James Garvey
>2005 *The Great Philosophers: From Socrates to Foucault.*
>New York: Barnes and Noble.

Tawney, R. H.
>1954 *Religion and the Rise of Capitalism.* New York: Mentor
>Books.

Thornton, Bruce
>2000 *Greek Ways: How the Greeks Created Western
>Civilization.* New York: M J F Books.

Van Gelder, Graig
>1996 "Mission in the Emerging Postmodern Condition," in *The
>Church Between Gospel and Culture: The Emerging Mission in
>North America.* George R. Hunsberger and Craig Van Gelder,
>eds. Grand Rapids: Eerdmans.

Todd, Richard A.
>1990 "Constantine and the Christian Empire," in *Introduction
>to the History of Christianity.* Tim Dowley, ed. Minneapolis:
>Fortress.

Weber, Max
>1958 *The Protestant Ethic and the Spirit of Capitalism: The
>Relationships Between Religion and the Economic and Social
>Life in Modern Culture.* New York: Scribner's.

Wedin, Michael V.
>1999 "Aristotle," in *The Cambridge Dictionary of Philosophy.*
>Robert Audi, ed. Cambridge: Cambridge University Press.

William, Barnard,
>1967 "Descartes, René," in *The Encyclopedia of Philosophy.*
>Paul Edwards, ed. New York: McMillan.

Williams, Robert Lee
>1999 "Persecution," in *Encyclopedia of Early Christianity.*
>Everett Ferguson, ed. New York: Garland.

LaVergne, TN USA
23 August 2009
155600LV00003B/7/A